POOLE
TOWN AND HARBOUR

BY RICHARD BLOMFIELD

Illustrations collected
and captioned by **Rodney Legg**

dpc
Dorset Publishing Company
at the Wincanton Press, National School, North Street, Wincanton, Somerset BA9 9AT

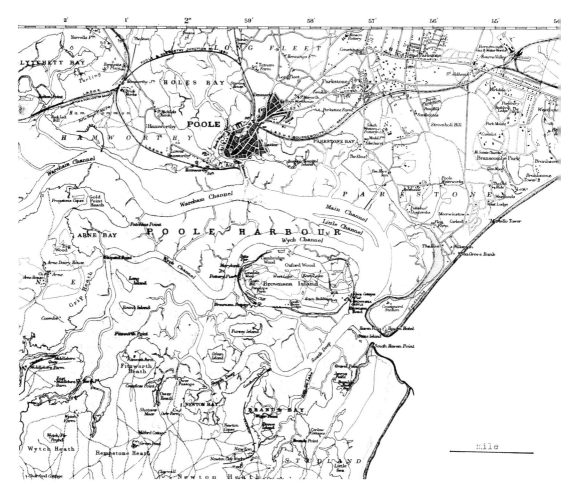

Map of Poole area at the completion of the late Victorian burst of railway building, showing lines converging on Hamworthy Junction. Both sets of track that pass northwards off the map (Castleman's Corkscrew in the west; the Somerset and Dorset at Stanley Green) have been closed and lifted, as has the mineral line at Hamworthy. The map is by W.H. Everett and Son, 13a Salisbury Street, London EC, and was published in 1890.

Publishing details. First published 1989 with main text © Richard Blomfield 1989 and captions © Rodney Legg 1989. Copyright of the photographs remains with the photographers.
Printing credits. Typesetting input by Reg Ward at Holwell, Dorset, and output at St Aldhelm's Road in Branksome, Poole, by Wordstream Limited. Screenprints of illustrations scanned by John Bull. Layout and design by Rodney Legg. Printed in Great Britain by Wincanton Litho at Wincanton Business Park, Wincanton, Somerset.
Distribution. By Dorset Publishing Company at the Wincanton Press, National School, North Street, Wincanton, Somerset BA9 9AT (telephone 0963 32583).
ISBN. International Standard Book Number 0 948699 14 0

A Profpect of the Town of POOLE from the Weft End of BRUNCKSEY ISLAND.

J. Bastard del.

A . Litchet Beacon	E . Upton	I . Keys
B . Roade to Wimborne	F . Oyster Bank	K . Heckford
C . Roade to Christchurch	G . Ham & Ham, Key	L . Parkson
D . Periams Ifland	H . Roap Walk	M . Road to Sturminfter.

J. Mynde fc.

This engraving of the Poole panorama, as seen from the west end of 'Bruncksey Island' – Brownsea Island – appears on page 3 of the main text of the first edition of John Hutchins's 1774 'History and Antiquities of the County of Dorset'. It is at the head of his account of the 'Peculiar of Canford' which is sub-headed 'The County, Town, and Borough of Poole'. The print shows (A) Beacon Hill, Lytchett Minster, at the west; (B) the road to Wimborne; (C) the road to Christchurch; (D) Pergins Island, which draughtsman John Bastard calls 'Periams Island', in Holes Bay; (E) Upton; (F) Oyster Bank off the east side of the Quay, since reclaimed; (G) Hamworthy village, left, and Hamworthy Quay, to the right; (H) Rope Walk, Lower Hamworthy; (I) Poole Quay and the bend around to West Quay; (K) Heckford, between Longfleet and Fleets Bridge; (L) Parkstone; (M) the road to Sturminster Marshall. There was a windmill on the eastern extremity of the spit, since reclaimed and infilled back to the town, to the south of what is now Poole Park.

Contents

Canford manorial roll — Poole did not become an independent town until 1248.

OPPOSITE

Poole Quay and Thames Street, drawn by Frank Short in 1884. This etching, courtesy Don L. Salter of British Columbia, shows the late sixteenth century King Charles tavern — which was named the New Inn after its Victorian renovation. It is now the King Charles again, but there has been some doubt over which Charles; Charles II of England visited Poole in 1665 and Charles X of France arrived as an exile in 1830. Not that there is much cause for uncertainty. The English were too Anglophobic to have considered, even in jest, the naming of a public house for a deposed French monarch.

Poole's first bridge, in Philip Brannon's print of about 1860, shows what was then being decried as a 'rickety alien abortion'. The townspeople had been thankful enough, however, when their MP and lord of the manor, Canford estate owner W.F.S. Ponsonby, paid for its erection in 1837. It is seen from Poole Quay, with Hamworthy on the other side of the water. A metal replacement would be provided in 1885.

THE WATER-DWELLERS

AT THE summit of Evening Hill a visitor from far inland halts to drink in the view. It is breathtaking. The great expanse of landlocked water is grey, green, blue or sand-coloured according to the depth and variegation of the sea bed. Its numberless bays and creeks are bordered with reeds and heather, and several islands are set within it.

As if this panorama were not rich enough, there stretches away to the south the open sea, surf breaking over the Hook Sands, and Studland Bay cupped in its arc of white cliffs. Little Sea shines in the middle of the moors between harbour and sea.

A massive, shallow-draught merchant vessel is nosing her way rather cautiously through the winding channel to the Port of Poole. It is a Truckline ship from Cherbourg, one of those which run as regularly as a bus service three times a day. Yet it is only a modern development of the way Poole has lived through the centuries, trading with those neighbours across the water in Brittany and Normandy from which some of its earliest inhabitants came.

The harbour's lack of depth has set limits to its commercial development, to the benefit of its wildlife, nature-lovers and yachtsmen. The flat-bottomed "Poole punt" used by today's harbour fishermen is the direct descendant of the dugout canoe salvaged from the mud off Brownsea Island in 1964 and believed to date from about 300 BC. As far as can be ascertained it measured thirty-three feet in length and had a draught of just under one foot. It was fashioned from an oak trunk measuring some five feet six and three-quarter inches in diameter, so the width of the canoe amidships would presumably have been about five feet. It could have been paddled by a crew of eighteen at a good speed and have carried turf, peat or stone. It was a boat suitable for shallow and protected waters.

This primitive dugout was built by the Durotriges, a Celtic tribe whose civilisation flourished in Wessex before the advent of the Romans. It was the fleet of their cousins the Veneti of Britanny that Caesar's fleet defeated in 56 BC off the French coast. He wrote admiringly of their sturdy seagoing ships, built of oak and bolted with iron. After this naval defeat, some of the Veneti may have settled in the Poole area, there to merge with the Durotriges, whose name means water-dwellers, and which evolved into that of Dorset. Their main settlement was at Hamworthy, just west of Poole, and they seem to have been a community of farmers and craftsmen who used ox-drawn carts and built an extensive network of roads. Like the modern English they loved horses. The bond was so strong that they used them in ritual sacrifices. In various parts of Dorset the bones of horses and humans have been found buried together, the horse sometimes being in full harness. Thus our links with north-western France go back to prehistory.

At Hamworthy the chief memorial to the Roman presence is the remains of a hard road which linked up with Ackling Dyke near Badbury Rings. To the Romans, Poole was a convenient port from which to send supplies inland to their army posts. Pottery too was sent north. Stone slates from Purbeck were used in villas at Dewlish and Tarrant Hinton, and its marble as far off as Colchester. The Roman conquest in Dorset was swift and violent, but after that our region was relatively peaceful during the Roman occupation.

Other finds besides the road were made in the Hamworthy area: a potter's kiln, several complete pots, coins, beads, iron objects and a fine specimen of a handmill for grinding corn.

> *The Romans threw us a road a road*
> *And sighed and strolled away.*
> *The Saxon gave us a raid a raid*
> *A raid that came to stay;*
> *The Dane went west but the Dane confessed*
> *That he went a bit too far.*
> *It was all the same for we all became*
> *The marvellous mugs we are ...*

Probably the Durotriges would have wished the Chestertonian view of history were more literally true. After the Romans, the Saxons and the Normans, and although the main tides of invasion tended to by-pass Poole, there were occasions when the Celts on this side of the Channel sought refuge with those across the water. At other times the Veneti came to the aid of the Dorset branch of the family when the Saxons were harassing them. On the other hand, there is evidence of intermixing between the new invaders and the Romano-British.

Times were harder for the inhabitants of the Isle of Wight, twenty miles across the water. Angles, Saxons and Jutes slaughtered them: but then came the Danes, who took a special fancy to Wessex. They arrived here in the late ninth century and chose to operate from Wareham, already fortified with massive earthworks and protected on two sides by the little rivers Frome and Piddle. King Alfred dared not attack and paid them 'Danegeld' to go away. But they stayed for a year, then moved to Exeter where they dug in and waited for supplies to arrive by sea. These were on their way when the English Channel, that temperamental stretch of water, threw one of its ugliest moods. A ferocious storm destroyed one hundred and twenty ships off Swanage. It seems likely that they were caught in the kind of short, steep seas that get thrown up over Peveril Ledges. Following this setback, the invaders did, for the time being, leave Wessex. But one hundred and twenty years later they were back in force, to avenge a massacre of their garrison by Ethelred. According to Holinshed the Danes sailed up the Frome with two hundred ships "royally decked", and by 1015 King Cnut from his stronghold in Wessex ruled England, Denmark and Norway.

The troubled times of Wareham, the forerunner of Poole as east Dorset's main port, were not over. Little more than a hundred years later it was Stephen, a son of William the Conqueror, who embroiled the little town in bloodshed and destruction. His feud was against the barons, the clergy and the rival claimant to the throne, Matilda. The result was that Wareham was almost destroyed in 1140. In spite of this, it continued as the chief port of the area for another fifty years.

The decline of Wareham has been attributed to three causes: the silting up of the Frome estuary, the devastation of the town in war, and the ambition of the Lord of the Manor of Canford to have a seaport of his own. As large ships were sailing up to Wareham four hundred years later, the depth of the river would seem to have little to do with it. Another suggestion is that the prevailing westerly winds made Wareham an awkward place to get to, as indeed it must have been in the sailing craft of the time. One marvels how so much commerce was accomplished, but accomplished it was; and the main reason for the port of Poole arising from the waves was probably the ambitions of the Earls of Salisbury, ten miles away at Canford, twice as far as Poole.

Not only is the early history of Poole bound up with the fact that it was a village within the great manorial settlement of Canford; its later development was often affected by relations with the lords of the Manor who owned the surrounding lands. Today the positions are reversed, with Canford a village overshadowed by the thrusting commercial town to the south and threatened by the spread of Bournemouth's suburbs from the east. But in mediaeval times Canford was the centre, Poole a small satellite and Bournemouth non-existent. Pleasantly situated in the fertile valley of the river Stour, Canford takes its place in history as the seat of the Earls of Salisbury, who owed their existence to William the Conqueror. Their main 'seat' was at Salisbury, although they owned fifty-one other manors around the country.

As detailed in the Domesday Book, the manor of Canford consisted of 2,160 acres of arable land, possibly two and a half square miles of pasture, one hundred and eighteen acres of meadow and nearly a square mile of woodland. The usual mediaeval hierarchy was tied to this estate, from villeins to slaves and including a smith, two millers, a mason, two carpenters and some bee-keepers. From the shores of Poole Harbour came the vital commodity of salt. It was shipped from Ower, on the opposite side of the harbour from Poole, where thirteen men were employed in the process of salt extraction, which involved the use of shallow iron pans. It was used to preserve meat. Later, in the twelfth century, the business of salt production was switched right across the harbour to Sterte, now on the outskirts of Poole. This was not only nearer to Canford but avoided the payment of rent.

The little town of Poole on its sandy, marshy peninsula could not on its own support a vicar, so he drew tithes from Longfleet and Parkstone as well. A 'tithe' meant one-tenth; and from Poole itself he was entitled to that percentage of its "barns, gardens, pigeon-houses, corn, grain, hay, wool, flax, hemp, lambs, fruits and profits".

A relic of those distant days is the building now known as Scaplen's Court, formerly the Old Town House. A detailed account of it is given in Chapter Four. At Canford the church was built by the end of the fourteenth century, and so was John of Gaunt's Kitchen, a name of mysterious origin. It is now a library in the school to which the manor house was converted in 1923. One of the 'kitchen's' massive fireplaces measures eighteen feet across.

The exact date of the beginnings of the port of Poole is unknown; but in the late eleventh or early twelfth century some sort of landing facilities were established on a spit of land outside the entrance to the present quays. It was called Baiter, which is still the name of this area which has become an extension of Poole Park. The shallow lagoon on the landward side has now been filled in, but until that happened Baiter was a little peninsula. It was the beginning of the rise of Poole and the decline of Wareham.

Having acquired his port, William Longespee, Lord of the Manor of Canford, allowed Poole to buy itself out of his control. This son of Henry II was a dedicated Crusader and badly needed money to finance his exploits. The sum agreed on was seventy marks. Exactly what this would mean in present-day money is difficult to estimate. One local historian suggested £500 in 1952. Another estimated £5,000 in 1972. In any case, Longespee got his money from the merchants of Poole and set off on an Anglo-French expedition. A detachment of the crusaders attacked the Turkish castle of Mansura and found themselves trapped inside the walls. Longespee was hacked to pieces and the leader of the Crusade, the brother of Louis IX of France, also died in this minor bloodbath. The mother of the fighting Lord from Canford had a memorial to him placed in Salisbury Cathedral.

Undoubtedly the merchants of Poole got the better of the bargain. The first sentence of the Longespee Charter reads:

"Know those present and those to come that I William Longespee have given and granted and by this my present charter have confirmed for me and mine heirs to my burgesses of Poole and their heirs all manner of liberties and free customs and aquittances as well of their bodies as of their goods from toll and all other customs and suits to be done without my borough of Poole to me or mine heirs belonging as the free citizens or burgesses of the cities or boroughs of the lord the King have throughout all England as fully as to me or my predecessors or heirs in any manner was known to belong through all my land sea ports and passages saving to me and mine heirs for every ship going to foreign parts beyond the seas two shillings." Half a dozen or so further sentences follow, some even longer than the first. However, the results of this baffling maze of verbiage were clear enough: what Poole gained was exemption from the levy of two shillings on every ship leaving for foreign ports and from rents formerly payable to absent bailiffs unconcerned with the day-to-day business of Poole.

The Longespee Charter dates from 1248. Stage by stage, over the next 300 years the growing importance of Poole was recognised by further legislation relating to its rights and status.

In 1364 Poole's history suddenly becomes linked with that of Winchelsea, which strikes one today as an odd partnership, since the Sussex village has been left a mile inland by a changing coastline and can hardly claim any particular importance. However, it used to be one of the famous Cinque Ports, those harbours and bases around the south-east corner of England, strategically placed with regard to France and enjoying certain privileges. This special status and power aroused rivalry and jealousy. There were violent clashes at sea between Poole-based ships and those from neighbouring ports such as Southampton as well as with others from the Cinque Ports. In the Winchelsea Certificate the Mayor and Barons of Winchelsea address themselves to their "dear friends and allies" the Mayor and Burgesses of Poole and grant it equal status with the more privileged ports. The next step came in 1411 when all the rights granted by previous charters were confirmed by the Lord of the Manor of Canford, Thomas Montacute, fourth Earl of Salisbury. Like the crusading Longespee he was a keen military man who took part in the siege of Orleans. The defences were in the charge of none other than Joan of Arc, and Thomas received a fatal wound in the face. Still, he earned a mention in Shakespeare's *The First Part of Henry the Sixth*.

Henry VI himself did even more for Poole, or 'Pole' as they called it, when he issued a Royal Charter allowing the local authorities to build fortifications and granting trading rights equal to those of Southampton. This meant that Poole was to be a staple port, with control of the most important cargoes, such as wool, leather and tin. The Mayor and his officers could now bypass remote bureaucrats and speed the processes of commerce. However, little advantage seems to have been taken of the permission for Poole to "wall, embattle and fortify itself". They relied mainly on a dyke, a gate and the surrounding mud.

About 1433 the building known as the Town Cellars was erected to store "commodities of the staple", mainly wool. Early records call it the Woolhouse. It was originally one hundred and twenty feet long, but Thames Street was driven through it. The design of two of its windows has given rise to the suggestion that this building had some religious connection, but in fact similar windows have been found in many other commercial buildings. More details about the Town Cellars will be found in Chapter Four.

The kings of mediaeval England were for ever making demands for men, money and ships to further their military ambitions, or else they were making feverish preparations to repel invaders. Edward III instituted the system under which every seaport sent a representative to London to give him an account of the number, type and condition of ships for which it could be held responsible. His aim was tighter control over England's maritime resources – a control by no means easy to achieve in those days of primitive communications. Poole had already shown itself capable of putting up stubborn resistance to kingly demands for men and ships. In the reign of Edward I it had refused to supply one ship to help suppress a rebellion by the Scots and Welsh. Thirty years later the growing port did provide four ships at the siege of Calais; but again at the time of the Spanish Armada Poole pleaded inability to swell the English fleet on the grounds that pirates based on Studland had caused crippling damage to Poole-based ships. Even in the eighteenth century there were to be sea-captains who refused to have their ships pressed into service.

In 1568 the population of the town was found to be 1,373. This is almost the same as it was estimated to be a hundred years earlier, the lack of increase being partly due to the ravages of the plague. There were epidemics in 1348 and 1361 and it took at least a hundred years for the losses to be made good. Apparently Baiter peninsula itself, the site of the original Poole Quay, was used as a burial ground.

Henry VI, who created Poole a staple port, also in 1453 established its trade fairs. At these gatherings merchants could exchange both goods and ideas and enjoy benefits similar to those provided by our modern international exhibitions. The historian H.P.Smith suggests that in the fifteenth century Poole was a bustling and prosperous town with "teams of flock-masters from the Dorset downs labouring beneath their packs and making their way to the quay ... business around the Woolhouse with galleys from Venice and broad-beamed caravels, Flemish as well as Poole vessels lying at the quayside; little taverns and cookshops alive with the chatter of woolfactors, flockmen and porters and the like". At the trade fairs, held twice a year, there would be "long rows of wooden booths on waste ground within the town limits and pack-horses, carts and wagons arriving with commodities for sale". One of the rules was that foreigners must buy from Poole merchants while the locals had to patronise the visiting merchants. There would be on sale wines, textiles, spices, leather goods, pots and pans; and during the sixteen days of the two fairs all shops were closed. Entertainments included bear-baiting, juggling and dancing.

Other occasions on which the outside world broke into Poole's self-contained existence were the Manorial Courts, held six times a year. One of their objects was the payment to the Lord of the Manor the sum of six shillings and eightpence to affirm the rights granted to Poole by the Charter of 1371. Records of these courts tell us that two men were fined threepence each for assaulting another, while a shipowner was ordered to remove his vessel from Poole Quay, where it had lain long enough to become a nuisance.

Law Courts were also held at Canford where tithes were collected and justice dispensed. In 1472 Kinson paid seven shillings, Canford six shillings and eightpence and Longfleet one shilling and threepence. Fines were imposed for poaching, neglect of property and other minor offences. Serious crimes were dealt with by a higher court.

The country as a whole was little affected by the Wars of the Roses, but naturally the Lords of the Manor of Canford felt their impact. The ownership of the Manor changed several times, sometimes reverting to the Crown until a new heir was chosen. Among them was the Earl of Warwick and when he was imprisoned Canford was given to his mother. Thus up to the end of the fifteenth century the Manor of Canford and with it the port of Poole were parcels of land to be fought over, exploited and given away by unscrupulous lords. According to a Reeve's account in the late 15th century, Poole, Upton and Hamworthy paid to the Manor of Canford the sum of £13.l7s.8d. per year, or in one particular year. Lord Stoughton, the Steward of the estate and its most highly-paid official, received £2.10s. "for the first moiety of the year", making an annual salary of £5. In those days a pig is estimated to have cost two shillings and a cockerel fourpence.

The trade fairs and the weekly market brought to Poole riches from abroad and from the fertile hinterland of Dorset. The ships at the quay were laden with goods from abroad and from other parts of England. Every visiting ship was charged twopence for anchorage. Dutiable goods included salmon, salt, salt fish, oil, wool, coal, tar, pitch, nuts, iron staves and skins. But mediaeval Poole was not a community composed entirely of respectable, law-abiding traders, fishermen and sailors: that would be a one-sided picture.

There were highwaymen on the roads and pirates at sea. It might be said that Poole was part of England's Wild West and the English Channel something akin to the streets of Chicago in the days of Al Capone. And if Poole provided no great admirals during the heroic ages of England, it at least has the distinction of having been the home of Harry Paye, the most notorious pirate of his age. He flourished in the late fourteenth and early fifteenth centuries and made his headquarters on Round Island, the most remote of those islands in the harbour which have deep water access. Any vessel approaching it would have a very good chance of running aground, especially at low water or on a falling tide.

Harry Paye attacked not only ships but seaports, anticipating the style of Drake, and took prisoners in France and Spain and held them to ransom. In 1407 he is reported to have brought 120 captured ships into Poole from Brittany, with cargoes of salt, iron, oil and wine. Three years earlier he had put in to the Isle of Wight with a Spanish prize and sent the crew back to France in small boats. Yet he seems to have spent almost as much time as a legitimate naval commander as he did in piracy. In 1404 he was serving with a squadron under Lord Berkeley and Sir Thomas Swynburn, who defeated a French force of which fourteen ships were put out of action. Again under Lord Berkeley in 1405 he intercepted a French naval fleet on its way to support Owen Glendower, the Welsh patriot, and destroyed fifteen ships.

In 1406 the French and Spaniards took their revenge by launching a surprise attack on Poole. The inhabitants were driven onto Canford Heath, part of the town was burned and some prisoners taken. Harry Paye's brother was killed, but the chief pirate himself was once again at sea with the navy, and so escaped. This Jack Tar of all trades would even sail pilgrims to the shrine of St James in Northern Spain if he had nothing more profitable to occupy him.

In the continual skirmishes between the French and the English at sea, sometimes the one side came off best, sometimes the other. In 1371 a famous French sailor, John le Vienne, raided the English coast and Poole was one of the towns he looted. The English expected a full-scale invasion to follow, but it never came. All round the coast stood beacons ready to be lit – posts topped with brush and a ladder up the side. They remained unused. A manuscript of 1544 in the Poole Corporation archives includes a list of "all ther namys that of owlde tyme have been accustomyd and ought to fynd hoblers to kepe the watche, in the tyme of warre, at the beken called Werybarowe."

A 'hobler' was a horseman and the beacon serving Poole may have been referred to in the passage quoted above. 'Werybarowe' has been assumed to have been a spelling of 'Worbarrow', a bay some sixteen miles down the coast from Poole entrance, but it is hardly likely that Poole would have been served by a beacon so far away and screened by the Purbeck Hills when there were several beacons in the Canford Cliffs-Bournemouth area.

The beacons were a part of the national defences renewed or initiated by Henry VIII. The ruthless but gifted monarch ordained that every man under sixty must have bows and arrows continually ready. Even boys over seven had to learn to shoot. A store of muskets and gunpowder was kept at Poole. The blockhouse on Brownsea Island was part of a chain of coastal defences which Henry VIII had built along the Hampshire and Dorset coasts. These included Studland Castle overlooking Poole Bay, Hurst Castle at the gateway to the Solent, and similar blockhouses at Southsea, Cowes, Calshot, Portland and Sandsfoot at Weymouth, and Yarmouth Castle.

Henry also helped Poole a little further along the road to independence by the issue of a Charter in 1526 which exempted the town from the powers of the High Court of Admiralty. It gave the Mayor of Poole, who had acted as Admiral "tyme out of mynde", the power to apprehend felons, pirates and other wrongdoers, to check goods found floating or salvaged and see that fishing regulations were obeyed. Mussels as well as oysters were conserved by forbidding the taking of the shellfish in its early stages. Fishermen were also forbidden to "suffer any Engynnes to lye in the sea" on Sundays.

No fixed dates were given when the Court was supposed to sit, but its location was to be at Broomhill, on the south side of Wareham Channel. It was the job of the Water Bailiff to publicise the forthcoming session of the

Court and to appoint twenty-four jurors. Its functions have been largely taken over by today's Harbour Commissioners.

As to punishments, in addition to fines, the stocks and the ducking-stool were commonly in use. The last-named was a chair on the end of a beam which overhung the quay.The victim was lowered into the water on the see-saw principle. The local Poole name for this apparatus was "clonking stool". To be ducked or 'clonked' was the accepted penalty for nagging women, or 'scolds'.

A regular feature throughout the town's historical records are the accounts of expenditure on the Mayor's entertainments, especially the dinners given annually and on special occasions. In 1511 the items listed include a 'kercher' for the Mayoress costing twenty shillings. This was a head-dress which at that price would have been the equivalent of a model gown from one of our top fashion houses. The routine of everyday life would also be lightened by occasional visits by companies of strolling players and by minstrels. On one occasion six shillings and eight pence was paid to a Cornish minstrel who "went about the town in the mornings and evenings".

The measure of autonomy granted to Poole by Henry VIII was small compared with the new powers established under the Charter of Elizabeth I in 1568. Of this event H.P.Smith writes: "It has always been to me a cause of wonder as well as of pride that the little port of Poole – a place of less than fourteen hundred inhabitants – should have won from Queen Elizabeth that 'Great Charter' which created it a county corporate distinct from the county of Dorset. At the time this Charter was granted there were only sixteen towns throughout the realm which had been raised to the dignity of county corporates."

The Charter cost Poole £500 and no doubt the Queen, the Privy Council and the merchants of Poole all considered they had a reasonable bargain.

The Charter enabled Poole to "purchase and possess all manner of goods, lands, tenements, liberties and hereditaments whatsoever". The Mayor and Bailiffs were empowered to arrest all manner of felons and commit them to gaol, and to levy taxes for local use. Poole was to be "one entire county" distinct from Dorset. And who was to wield power over this county? The burgesses, successful merchants who had become a self-perpetuating governing clique. Now they could appoint a Sheriff to be responsible for the town gaol and to superintend executions.

The Sheriff of Poole is still an important person, especially with regard to the processes of law and the entertainment of visiting legal dignitaries. Another privilege granted under the Charter was that Poole ships no longer had to pay quay dues when visiting other English ports, an exemption also enjoyed by Southampton.

A new "Town House" was now needed and a new prison: and a single building was used for both purposes, the prison being on the lower floor of an establishment sited in what is now Castle Street.

Scaplen's Court, drawn by Sheila Sturdy in 1949. The collapse of a chimney in 1923 revealed fifteenth century walls, seen here after the later layers of building had been stripped. Subsequently, the Sarum Street frontage has been restored into a full-size replica of a mediaeval town house.

SPANIARDS and SMUGGLERS

CONTINUALLY AGGRAVATED by English depredations on Spanish shipping both by pirates and naval adventurers, Philip of Spain prepared his great Armada and sent it on its mission of revenge and religious conversion in 1588. Long accustomed to living under the threat of invasion, England was ready. The beacon system was arranged so that reinforcements could immediately be summoned from inland, every man and boy was trained in archery, and the less able-bodied were organised into the Elizabethan equivalent of the Home Guard of the 1939-45 war.

Poole, however, did not live up to this high standard of preparedness. The Commission in charge of defence wrote to the Privy Council that the town was poorly defended, the best men were away at sea and no tax for the mustering of soldiers had been paid.

There were seven forts along the Dorset coast – Brownsea, Studland, Sandsfoot and Portland castles, Handfast and Peveril Points and St Alban's Head. The last three were blockhouses with room for a gunner to lie. Most if not all of these strategic points would be refortified in 1940. Weymouth grudgingly supplied two ships to the English fleet. Poole eventually provided one, despite the attempt of a pro-Spanish Catholic to bribe the captain to stay out of the fight.

The Armada set sail on 30 May 1588, a fleet of one hundred and thirty ships carrying 30,000 men. Among them were nearly two hundred monks and friars, who would later carry their message to the English. Through the fleet the password was changed daily, from Jesus to Holy Ghost to Holy Trinity, and through to Our Lady on Saturdays.

The commanders in Dorset were Sir Henry Seymour, Sir Richard Rogers, Sir John Horsey, Thomas Howard and George Trenchard. As the Spanish fleet passed majestically along the Channel from west to east in its favoured crescent formation, each port feared it might be the one selected for invasion. But the massive wooden walls passed on, harassed by the smaller English ships. The design of these ships, both their hulls and their armament, was at this period ahead of the rest of Europe. The English ships not only had greater speed but better ability to get to windward. For three days the Spanish fleet passed along the Dorset coast and two battles developed, the first off Portland. The duel swung to and fro a few miles from the shore, where guns were positioned and soldiers waited. When the ships disengaged, small boats from Dorset and Hampshire ports hurried forth with food, water and munitions. One of the ships involved was the *San Salvador*. It was brought into Weymouth where some of the crew were imprisoned. Among them was a woman whose nature and origins are a mystery.

The Privy Council decided to transfer the *San Salvador* to Portsmouth and she was taken in tow with that object, but she sank in Studland Bay. Out of a crew of fifty-seven an English warship rescued thirty-four. The wreck is presumed still to be at the bottom of the sea off Studland.

Brownsea Island enjoyed a similar independence to that of Poole, but under the threat of invasion the Privy Council put a stop to the negligent and wayward lifestyle of the islanders. Sir Richard Rogers was given authority over the Purbeck area and he had men and arms sent to Brownsea.

The Armada proceeded slowly westwards until it was off the Purbeck coast, while the land forces kept pace with it, the soldiers following coastal tracks to Wareham and Poole. The battle in these waters raged for two hours and included a duel between Drake's *Revenge* and the *Gran Grifón* which left the Spanish ships disabled. The Spanish commander, the Duke of Medina Sidonia, "struck his topsails", which means he lowered them, the nautical equivalent of throwing down the gauntlet. He had already made this chivalric gesture off Portland to no effect, and Drake again wisely declined to respond. He judged survival to be more important than adherence to the antique etiquette of battle.

The wind dropped. The Spanish fleet drifted south of the Isle of Wight, shadowed by the English. Again the small boats darted out from the neighbouring harbours to bring provisions and ammunition. A ship called the *Anne Royal* is known to have been supplied with powder by a boat from Poole. Everybody wanted to play a part and young men who could afford to do so hired boats and set forth to join the fleet. The Spaniards made for Calais to link up with the Duke of Parma, who was to provide barges to be towed across the Channel laden with soldiers. The English fleet which pursued them now included privateers and armed merchant vessels numbering over a hundred, besides regular warships. It must have been a daunting sight. The great naval battles developed off the French and Dutch coasts. It seemed that the Spanish fleet must be driven on to the Zeeland Banks, but a last-minute shift of wind saved them. But no Spanish ship escaped damage, whereas the English suffered little. And now the elements, which had twice saved the Spaniards, did the reverse. Westerly gales lashed them and brought them to a standstill. Perhaps as many as seventeen of their fleet reached the coast of Ireland, only to be slaughtered by the English garrison. Others were wrecked on the Scottish coast, yet the Duke of Medina Sidonia succeeded in leading sixty-six of his ships back to Corunna. These included two-thirds of the fighting ships.

Typhus and scurvy were rampant through both fleets, and after the great victory had been won, the sight of crippled heroes became common in many coastal towns. Yet the Elizabethan age was not unmindful of the need for social welfare. A levy in aid of the poor was enforced under an Act of 1572. Under the Poor Law Act of 1601 every parish was obliged to appoint an Overseer whose job it was to see that the needy and homeless were cared for and trained in houses of correction. Homeless children were to be given refuge and so were vagrants. An interesting distinction was made between lazy tramps and those who were 'impotent', meaning helpless. On arrival at a house of correction the lazy ones were whipped before being fed and given work.

Poole already had the Almshouses of St George, built in the reign of Henry V and bought by the Corporation in 1550. Rogers Almshouses were built in 1604. Rogers is a famous name in Poole history. The 1574 census records three families of that name. As described in Chapter Four, Woodes Rogers, author, navigator and Governor of the Bahamas, came from Poole. The founder of the Almshouses was Robert Rogers who became a prosperous leather merchant in London, left over £3,000 to a variety of charities and "500 marks to build an alms house to house six poor couple ... or to such others as shall have most need of relief". These couples were also to receive twelve pence per week. In 1852 six further cottages were added to the row of Rogers Almshouses and the whole block was reconditioned in 1927. On a certain day during the early 1600s forty-one people are listed as having received bread, though they do not include those living in the almshouses. One-tenth of a quarter of all grain shipped from Poole was put aside for the poor. The Mayor was responsible for managing his budget as best he might. He would see that the quays and roads were properly maintained and undertake other public works, but if he could contrive a surplus he might feel quite justified in organising some lavish entertainments. The expenditure for a year in the early 17th century totalled £40, and an election celebration itemised four pigs at 4 shillings, 1½ dozen chickens at 3s.9d., four dozen butter at 11s.6d., six couple of rabbits at 5 shillings; also sugar, spices, currants, marmalade and much else totalling £10.2s.7d. – nearly a quarter of Poole's annual income.

In 1563 the Mayor was Thomas Byngley. His revenue came to £18.16s.4d. while his expenditure was £70.14s.6d. "So the whole that the town oweth me is £51.18s.2d." An important part of the budget were the improvements made to the defences of Brownsea Castle including:

> *2 pairs of wheels for the ordnance £1.15s.0d.*
> *To George the gunner for one quarter's wages £2.5s.6d.*
> *To 4 men watching at Brownsea 14 days £1.17s.4d.*
> *For 2 cheeses, one doz. bread and a barrel of beer*
> *when the great brazen piece was set on its carriage at*
> *Brownsea ... £0.7s.6d.*
> *For half a hundred of lead to make shot £0.6s.8d.*

Baiter peninsula, so much a part of Poole and the place where the first quay arose, was still owned by the Lord of the Manor of Canford, and Thomas Byngley's budget includes two shillings for the rent for the Baiter, paid to the Reeve of Canford. As to law and order, the gulf between the outlook of our Elizabethan ancestors and our own is suddenly made vivid and real when the town accounts for 1524 include payments for a new pillory, stocks and ducking-stool. We are at one with them, however, in having experienced the threat of invasion. In 1589 Francis Hawley, the Governor of Corfe Castle, wrote to Poole's Mayor and Corporation: "I charge you in her Majesty's name ... that you suffer not any bark, ship or vessel to pass out your port other than in small vessels from port to port within this realm ... and if in any case you should find cause why then I ... require you to take away the sails of all such ships ..."

One year before the Armada, Sir Harry Ashley had also written to the Mayor of Poole concerning this question of "The Staye of Shipps": "I have sent to the Viceadmiral to make stay in every porte within the whole county of Dorset and have answer from his Wiffe that he is in Plymouthe ... This ffar ye well."

Queen Elizabeth was confronted by another problem closely connected with the defence of the realm, and that was piracy. The continual harassment of Spanish and French merchant vessels by the English was an embarrassment to the Queen in her attempts to keep the peace; and most of the distinguished men who played an honourable part in the defence of England against the Armada were deeply involved in piracy and smuggling. Empire-building and piracy were closely interwoven, and the Dorset coast offered splendid cover, with Poole as the most important base.

The campaign for what was called "The Reformation" of piracy was launched in 1577. In 1578 a letter from the Queen was addressed to "Our trustye and wellbeloved maior of our towne of Poole for the tyme being and to our dear cosens ..." There follow the names of the Marquis of Winchester, Lord Howard of Bindon, Sir Henry Ashley and seven other knights. Again in 1583 the Queen addresses "Our trustye and wellbeloved Mayor of the Towne and Countye of Poole for the tyme being, Giles Escorte Esquier Recorder of the same towne, William Newman, William Greene, John Rogers and William Dyker".

These worthy citizens were appointed Commissioners for the apprehension of pirates. They were required to appoint reliable men at every port and creek to keep watch on shipping. They were to obtain details of all ships within the last five years which had been equipped "in warlike manner and not in trade or merchandise without her Majesty's special licence". The port-watchers were also required to provide the names of ships' captains and riggers and details of prizes and cargoes, and to whom and where these had been sold.

If the Commissioners had carried out their task to the letter, the trail would have led them through the portals of every stately home in Dorset, including their own. Effective action could only come from the Privy Council and the Admiralty. In 1583 two government warships raided the Dorset coast with the result that forty-three pirates were brought to trial. The name of the new judge at the High Court of Admiralty was Julius Caesar, and in 1590 he was entertained at Poole.

Sir Richard Rogers of Bryanston was High Sheriff of Dorset in 1588 and in charge of the Blandford Division during the great invasion scare. His house was built from stones of Bindon Abbey, the ruins of which stand on the banks of the Frome at Wool. His brother Francis was his henchman in piracy, and other dignitaries involved were Sir Francis Hawley, who was Deputy Commandant of Corfe Castle, Sir Christopher Hatton, the Vice Admiral of Purbeck, and Christopher Anketill, who was in charge of Brownsea Castle. All these gentlemen had dealings with a pirate named Courte, who brought two captured French ships into Mupe Bay, near Lulworth. One of these ships was sailed to Poole by a servant of Sir Christopher Hatton named George Fox. Anketill bought goods from the captured ships, including wine, timber and furniture, and shipped them inland from different points in Poole Harbour.

As one of the recipients, Sir Richard Rogers was fined £100, a penalty which one may regard as a warning. Less distinguished and more expendable figures in such cases received harsher treatment. Seven well-known pirates were hanged at Wapping in 1578 "at the turn of the tide". In 1581 several pirates were hanged on Studland beach, a spectacle which the public considered excellent entertainment.

Robert Gregory was Member of Parliament for Weymouth/Melcombe and a Freeman of Poole. He was also a prosperous merchant dealing in pirated and smuggled goods. He was therefore well qualified to conduct inquiries into piracy, which was one of his jobs during his years at Weymouth, when he was Deputy Searcher, a sort of Customs officer who kept a check on imports.

The Deputy Searcher for West Lulworth revealed that the pirate Courte not only dined with Sir Richard Rogers but used to spend the night at the vicar's house. There is a record of a bible being presented to "parson Cook of Swanage" by a pirate named Vaughan, while from the same gentleman the Mayor of Poole received a pair of crimson silk stockings.

When eight men were arrested in Poole for piracy, the Mayor refused to give any help. His attitude was no doubt due at least in part to the sense of grievance felt by Poole men when the Queen deprived them of the Governorship of Brownsea and presented it to Sir Christopher Hatton. From their commanding position in the harbour mouth, the guardians of Brownsea could and did appropriate much of the pirated booty which had previously fallen to Poole. This rivalry between Poole and Purbeck again showed itself, and violently, when the gunners of Brownsea Castle fired on and damaged a ship which the Poole authorities had permitted to leave port, contrary to the urgent request of the Admiral of Purbeck.

Poole had its own Admiralty Court and clearly did make some effort to contribute to the anti-piracy campaign. The town accounts for 1581-82, when Christopher Farewell was Mayor, mention expenditure incurred in connection with the suppression of piracy. He spent "ij li. iiijs [£2.3s.?] Rydynge to London upon my horses and my selffe about the towne's busenes in S'VENGE to remove the haunte of the pirats from handfaste beenge for the space of xxij dais that is from the vij of Novembar to ye 8 of december".

Evidently Mr Farewell had to visit Stevenage to consult some official connected with the Commission for the Apprehension of Pirates. By 'handfaste' he must have meant the sheltered bay of Studland, which that exposed headland encloses, and the village itself, where several houses were in regular use by pirates.

The same accounts include:

> 'watching a prisoner at night 4d
> mending the butes [butts] 4s.
> beanes for mr. escottes & horses 4s.0d.

In 1585 the French ship *La Lune* was brought into Studland and burned. In a letter to the Mayor of Poole Lord Burghley recommends that Nicholas Curry "deserved to be recompensed" for helping to salvage the cargo of salt. Also that the ship be laid up safely out of reach of the French. Not a word about piracy. The commendation of Nicholas Curry is somewhat ironical since this individual four years earlier had led an agitation against the tax on beer, which was four shillings a 'brewlock' on beer bought from the "common brewers". The corporation's defence was that the money went towards numerous public works.

The sea bandits did not only prey upon foreigners. Ships from Scotland or from other English ports were all fair game to the privateer whose sole interest was in his own enrichment. In 1586 Harry Weller and Bonaventer Ande of Torbay and William Bonde of Milbrooke were attacked by pirates off Swanage. Weller was robbed of four barrels of herrings, an anchor, all the ship's 'apparel', 100 buckhorn and the ship's axe. Bonaventer lost 300 "dry newland fish" and a lantern. Bonde lost a quantity of "new powdered milwell and ling", a flag, a sounding line and a shirt.

It seems that the picture of the pirate popularised in boys' adventure stories is by no means totally untrue. Cruel and ruthless as he was, the piratical seaman had to be extremely hardy and able. He may well have often had a parrot perched on his shoulder and worn gaudy clothing. Scarlet was supposed to be the pirates' lucky colour and they often gave away parrots and monkeys as presents. Lord Howard of Bindon's cook acquired one of each in this way and some parrots found their way to Corfe Castle. Pirates dressed themselves and their women in the finest and brightest materials they could filch from the holds of French and Spanish merchantmen laden with silks and satins.

Queen Elizabeth's drastic action curbed piracy but by no means put an end to it. A hundred and forty years later Captain Woodes Rogers of Poole was mounting an equally efficient campaign to stamp out the pirates based on Bermuda. There were Barbary and Turkish pirates in the Mediterranean, while in the Channel French and English seamen carried on a continual guerilla warfare.

But now England was moving into a period during which the people of our country were to fight each other not only at sea but across the face of

England in civil war. Its outcome was to determine the history of England during the following centuries and start a revolution which led to the United Kingdom becoming the centre of world commerce and of financial and naval power.

The price of cod oil in this heyday of the Newfoundland fisheries was £25 a ton; so if one ship could bring back six tons it is no wonder that Poole had so many stately mansions to witness the fortunes made by the ship-owners. Their trade was by no means confined to fish and oil. Their ships exported the lowest grade fish to the slave plantations in the West Indies, the best quality to the Mediterranean countries, and brought back to England wine, oil, fine fabrics and fruit. The ships were lightly armed and some of the small cannon they carried may still be seen in gateways to yards on Poole Quay.

In the earlier days of the cod fishery both the Admiralty and the fish merchants had opposed any permanent settlement in Newfoundland. The country needed seamen and the merchants wanted a monopoly. Ship's masters were instructed not to leave men on the other side of the Atlantic. But then came the French bid for dominion over Canada and this policy had to go into reverse. As late a 1684 there were only one hundred and twenty settlers; in 1774 there were 12,000 and by 1804 the number had risen to about 20,000, largely made up of Irish immigrants. In fact the Poole merchants began to make permanent settlements along the Newfoundland coast as early as 1700, and so began the process by which England's first colony grew up to independence from the old country, just as all the other colonies were destined to do in the course of time. It would eventually join the Dominion of Canada in 1949.

Soon the great fishing families were building ships in Newfoundland – Kemp, Slade, Fryer, Gosse, Lester, Garland, Pack, Pike and Green – names still common on the other side of the water. The Spurriers had shipyards at Oderin and Burin and were building barques and brigs there. If they sent ships to England at all they preferred them to spend a whole year in Newfoundland instead of six months. St John's became a financial and distributive centre and by the end of the eighteenth century the old home-based system was already in a transitional state.

Other factors contributed to the strikingly sudden collapse of the great cod fishery. The Treaty of Amiens in 1802 ended the British monopoly in Newfoundland; Wellington's armies, numbering 300,000, whose rations had included salt fish, were disbanded; and Britain experienced a series of economic crises which seriously damaged the home market. Though Newfoundland contributed the greater part of Poole's fishing industry it was by no means the whole of it. There were local fish and above all there were oysters. The trade in the harbour's native wild oyster reached its peak in the early eighteenth century when thousands of barrels of pickled oysters were exported every year. Excavations on the Quay in 1885 revealed oyster shells to a depth of four feet.

The affluence of Napoleonic wartime came to a sudden end. In 1816 and subsequent years, poverty drove the working people to violent revolt in the big cities. They could not afford to buy the goods turned out by the factories, or even adequate food and clothing. The whole continent of Europe was similarly in the grip of recession and the great British export boom was halted.

The farmers were equally hard hit and England at this time was an overwhelmingly agricultural country. These hard times led to the Chartist Movement and the Anti-Corn Law League; and a few years later, in 1834, to Dorset's Tolpuddle Martyrs.

In these conditions it was less and less attractive to those engaged in the Poole-Newfoundland fishing business to trade with Europe and increasingly tempting to them to consolidate their foothold in North America. The result is written all too clearly in the figures for Poole-based fishing vessels during this period. In 1816 they numbered over three hundred; in 1828 less than twenty. Poole's greatest commercial venture had become a dwindling remnant.

French and American warships, pirates from France, North Africa and Turkey – all had battered continually at Poole's transatlantic fishing fleet, yet commerce with Newfoundland had continued to grow and flourish. For twenty-five years England was again under threat of invasion and the home defences were mobilised. The plan for Dorset "approved by his Majesty" (George III) included details for the organisation of wagons, horses, millers, bakers, cattle drivers, volunteer soldiers and the transport of live and dead animals. The volunteers were to bear arms, serve as guides, provide carts, grind corn, bake bread and provide boats. Men were divided into four classes: 1, between seventeen and thirty years old and unmarried; 2, between thirty and fifty; 3, between seventeen and thirty with not more than two children under ten; 4, all the others.

However, the fighting, as usual, took place overseas, and life at home carried on, enjoying the wartime boom, while even before the wars Poole seems to have been reasonably prosperous. *Bailey's British Directory of Merchants and Traders Useful Companion* of 1784 lists nine shipbuilders and seven sailmakers; two anchor makers and eleven surgeons. Going back to the beginning of the century, the Town Accounts for 1712 give an insight into changing customs. Items of expenditure include:

> *Ringing ye eight of Clock Bell*
> *The Cryer for people to cleane ye streets*
> *Repairing the Walk at the Great Quay and Whipping*
> *six mumpers [beggars]*
> *Rejoicings on the King's birthday*
> *The Trumpeter and for use of Javelins and other*
> *charges.*

A hundred years earlier a document records donations towards the building of a new quay: "A belevelence for the bylden of a newe keye at messerars Gape & a ffyshe markitt next yeare if God parmytts." A list of names of donors follows.

Records of Quarter Sessions reveal something of the everyday life of our ancestors. They had continual trouble over the disposal of rubbish and sewage, a heap of either of which was known as a 'mixon'. For example in 1767 Mrs Elizabeth Christian was 'presented' for "not raising the Chimney of her kitchen or Washhouse, it being so low that the sparks ... is in the most Eminent danger of setting fire to the straw and litter on the dung mixon of the Lion and Lamb Inn". In 1770 Mr Willis the schoolmaster is in trouble "for suffering his Schollars to do their necessary occasions against the old Town Hall being very great Nuisances, and desire it may not be done for the future". In 1742 Robert Randall had left "dung etc. round the post on the Little Ke which makes the post useless". Such offences all came under the heading of 'nuisance', and so did the failure of the ferryman to maintain a regular service "to carry passengers & ye inhabitants of ye said Town and County for ye passage from Poole to Ham".

A charge not heard today was brought in 1708 against one Elizabeth Serrell, accused of being "a common scold and abuser of her neighbours". "Cursing and swearing" was also an offence, the exact number of oaths being recorded. And pigs caused a lot of trouble through owners letting them go out of control. Strangely, the Mayor of Poole himself is several times among those 'presented' at Quarter Sessions. In 1765, for example, he is held responsible for the deplorable condition of Salisbury prison, which was "unfit to retain prisoners". In 1754 he is required to do something about the Little Key, part of which collapsed into the channel. On another occasion he is accused of driving in posts near the Key "to the danger of ships". In 1769 "His Worshipful the Mayor" is 'presented' for not "keeping up the stocks on the Key".

The latter part of the eighteenth century saw the rise of Poole's great merchant families in the Newfoundland fisheries. In the first half of the century one of Poole's most remarkable sons, Woodes Rogers, made his career. Hitherto some doubt had been expressed as to whether he came from Poole or Bristol. But a document of 1690 recording citizens who paid one shilling 'Poll Rate' includes the following: "Woodes Rogers, Frances his wife, Woodes their child." Since Woodes Rogers was born in 1679 it seems likely that he was born in Poole and was evidently there at the age of eleven.

In 1708 he set off on a privateering expedition, taking as pilot William Dampier, the explorer, author and buccaneer. Rogers took two ships, the *Duke* and the *Duchess*, was confronted with a mutiny, sailed round Cape Horn and put into the island of Juan Fernandez for rest and recuperation. They sent a pinnace ashore to reconnoitre. It came back with a man "clothed in goat skins who looked wilder than the first owners of them. He had been on the island four years and four months." It was Alexander Selkirk, who had remained on the island following a quarrel with his captain. He had previously sailed with Dampier and "agreed to be a mate aboard our ship". Back in England he became the original of Defoe's *Robinson Crusoe*. Woodes Rogers describes his two-year expedition in *A Cruizing Voyage Round the World* and gives a vivid account of the meeting with Selkirk. "We had a bulldog," he writes, "which we sent with several of our nimblest runners to help him in catching goats; but he distanced all and tired both Dog and the Men, catched the Goats and brought 'em to us on his back. He made fire "by rubbing two sticks of Piemento together on his knee". He built two huts roofed with goatskins and "in the lesser Hutt ... he dress'd his victuals, and in the larger he slept and employ'd himself in reading, singing psalms and praying". When he ran out of powder for his musket he caught goats "by speed of foot, for his continual Exercise of walking and running clear'd him of all gross Humours". The rats "gnawed at his feet and clothes while asleep, which obliged him to cherish the Cats with his Goat's-flesh; by which so many of them became so tame that they would lie about him in hundreds and soon delivered him from the rats. He likewise tamed some kids and to divert himself would now and then sing and dance with them and his Cats: so that by the Care of Providence and Vigour of his Youth, being now but about 30 years old, he came at last to conquer the Inconveniences of his Solitude, and to be very easy.

"He had so much forgot his language for want of use that we could scarce understand him, for he seemed to speak his words by halves. We offered him a dram, but he would not touch it, having drank nothing but water since his being there." Woodes Rogers concludes that the example of Alexander Selkirk, of Largs, Scotland, "may instruct us how much a plain and temperate way of living conduces to the Health of the Body and the Vigour of the Mind ... for this man, when he came to our ordinary Method of Diet and Life, though he was sober enough, lost much of his Strength and Agility. But I must quit these Reflections which are more proper for a philosopher and Divine than a Mariner ..."

Alexander Selkirk lived on to make many more voyages. The Woodes Rogers expedition came out at a handsome profit. "It cost less than £14,000 to fit out," says G.E. Mainwaring in his preface to the 1928 edition of *A Cruising Voyage*, and the net profits amounted to at least £170,000. The actual value of the plunder is stated in a contemporary petition to have amounted to £800,000. Every man who took part received a share. Two large candlesticks captured during the 'cruise' are now in Bristol Cathedral.

Rogers was a born leader besides being a magnificent seaman. His voyage with Dampier "opened a door to the great South Sea which was never to be closed again". Woodes Rogers retired to live in affluence for a few years, but came willingly out of retirement to lead an expedition to the Bahamas. There he brought order out of chaos, curbed the pirates and instituted proper government for the first time. Through all the bloody encounters at sea he had managed to part on good terms with his adversaries. Once a musket ball smashed his upper jaw, while another carried away part of an ankle bone. Without the aid of any but the crudest surgery he carried on and led his "cruising voyage" to a triumphant success. Woodes Rogers's father figures on one occasion in the annals of Poole: In 1688 he sued one Thomas Stevens for using "a rush cable", a rope of poor quality, to moor Rogers's ship *Endeavour*, which broke away and was lost.

Writing in the East Dorset Herald in 1916 Alderman Herbert Carter says that sailing vessels formerly engaged in the Poole-Newfoundland fisheries are still frequently to be seen at Poole Quay. He mentions one of only 80 tons. This yachtsman and sometime Mayor of Poole also recounts a story which makes a remarkable parallel with that of the *Marie Celeste*. It concerns a small trading schooner called the *Mountaineer*, owned by a well-known Poole family. "One fine summer day she left Poole for Labrador. Some weeks later she was found with all plain sail set, almost within sight of the American coast, her galley fire still smouldering, a meal spread in the cabin, but with no soul on board. The mystery remains unsolved. Neither boat nor men ever reached shore, nor was any reason discovered for the abandonment of a well-founded craft which continued trading for many years after the incident."

The author recounts another curious episode in the same article. A Poole ship was captured in the English Channel by a French privateer, but the Frenchman released his victim on finding that the Poole man was, like himself, a Mason. As a token of friendship the Frenchman hung a biscuit round the neck of the Englishman's dog and the Poole Masons, says Alderman Carter, "still preserve this interesting relic".

Poole tokens, issued when the nation ran out of change. This happened twice. The top two examples, in bronze, were minted in 1666 by trader 'Moses Durell of Poole' and the following year 'For the Mayor of ye Town and County of Poole'. By 1811 it was silver that was in short supply: 'Town and County of Poole Token − Value One Shilling − James Ferris, Silversmith, Poole.'

Roundheads (on the ladder) and Cavaliers fighting in Dorset, for Corfe Castle, in a print from Mary Palgrave's romantic Victorian adventure story 'Brave Dame Mary'. The besiegers in 1643 were from the Parliamentarian stronghold of Poole but the fortress did not fall until 1646. It was then reduced to a ruin, by undermining and packing charges of gunpowder, on orders from the House of Commons.

MAKING WAR and MAKING MERRY

IN MID-SEVENTEENTH century all Europe was in a state of crisis. The feudal system was breaking up and new forms of government had to be developed to meet the demands of a new merchant class and their expanding trade. The Dutch had begun to evolve the sort of system that was needed, but there were only about two million of them. In France the monarchy triumphed and the merchant classes had to accept a subordinate role. But in England between 1640 and 1660 a decisive struggle took place with the victory going the other way. Some kind of parliamentary government was assured and the base created from which the United Kingdom developed into the first great industrial nation and the most successful imperial power.

Before this could happen the absolute power of the King had to be broken. Charles I not only overruled Parliament but invaded the affairs of local authorities formerly controlled by officials such as JPs and Sheriffs. There was conflict over various taxes imposed by the King and a range of fines which included one for refusing to accept a knighthood and pay for it. A member of the Government, William Noy, discovered an old law which enabled the King to levy Ship Money not only on seaports but on towns far inland. Poole paid £60, Wareham £30, Corfe £10 and Dorset as a whole £5,000.

As the clash of interests intensified each side began to muster forces, and Oliver Cromwell emerged as the leader who chose "plain and godly men" with no pretensions to wealth or titles.

Dorset was divided over the Civil War, but Poole remained steadfastly on the side of Parliament. It is thought that Hamworthy church was pulled down so that the stones could be used to build defences. Poole may have praised God but it certainly believed in keeping its powder dry. Parliament helped by contributing four ships and some arms. Wareham was Royalist and so was Sherborne, from which stronghold the Marquis of Hertford tried to bribe and bully his way into Poole. He would, he said, spend £200 a week in the town if they would let him in. But the Mayor stood firm. His name was Henry Harbin, now commemorated in that of a well-respected school. These events took place in 1643, when a detachment from Poole spent six weeks battering at Corfe Castle, with no appreciable result. This attack was led by Sir Walter Erle, an ancestor of the family Erle Drax of Charborough Park, near Wareham, on which town Sir Walter was based. When a large Royalist force appeared near Dorchester, he abandoned the siege of Corfe and Wareham fell into Royalist hands. Poole Roundheads frequently raided the town, which finally fell to General Sir Ashley Cooper in 1644. The previous year, Parliament had sent the following directive to Sir Ashley: "You are desired forthwith to repair to the Isle of Purbeck and to draw together as speedily as may be out of the garrisons of Poole, Wareham, Lulworth and Weymouth such members of foot and horse as are sufficient to block up Corfe Castle." It fell in 1646 through treachery from within. The accounts of the Mayor of Poole for 1645-46 list items of expenditure on besieging the castle: 4 shs to the messenger who brought the news; 8 shs and 2d for faggots for the guards; and 4lbs of prunes for the gunners, costing 2 shs and 8d. Prunes also feature in the mayoral accounts for the years following the Civil War, when Poole was ravaged by bubonic plague: "A lb. of prunes for Hookey's wife - 2d." Mutton, broth and bread sent to the pest house, pots, pills, shrouds and "a bottle for smoking of houses" are other items bought for the unfortunate victims in a town where "plague and famine busily contend for pre-eminence and the distressed inhabitants ... threaten to break out to the ... ruin of places adjacent".

The Royalists under the Earl of Crawford tried to capture Poole by treachery. Captain Francis Sydenham of Poole was in debt and pretended to be willing to betray the town. The go-between was a Captain Phillips, a Royalist, or 'malignant' as the parliamentarians called them. "They began to treat of the manner how to betray the towne and the ship in Brownsea Roade and that he should be captain of the watch and the Earle to approach the towne with some troopes of horse in the dead of night and that the gate should be left open ..."

But Francis Sydenham turned the tables. The Earl and his party found themselves caught in a trap and one witness said that the dead would have filled "divers cartloades". However, the Royalist report put the number of dead at only ten. If that were correct it was probably because the guns covering the town gate were sited too high. Sydenham's trap was possible because Poole had to be entered across a narrow neck of land. The lagoon formed by Baiter peninsula had been filled in, another branch of this inlet was pushed back to create the lake in Poole Park while on the other side of the neck Holes Bav encroached further inland than it does today. Thus in earlier times the access route to the town was a strip of land no more than fifty yards wide. It could be sealed off by a gate supplemented with chains, while on either side of the gate was a crescent-shaped length of wall. An enemy intending to pass through the gate would find himself caught between stone pincers, the gap between which could be sealed off by chains.

The Phillips-Sydenham affair was described in a pamphlet published in 1643 and entitled "A true relation of a Plot to Betray the Towne of Poole in the County of Dorset. And likewise how many of the Conspirators were entrapped and cut off. And more particularly of the narrow escape of Lord Crawford. As it was presented to the House of Commons 29th September 1643."

Captain Francis Sydenham was at this time aged 26. In the same year he led a successful attack on Wareham. He was a member of the well-known Dorset family from Wynford Eagle, near Maiden Newton. His elder brother Colonel William Sydenham was a Governor of Melcombe Regis and Weymouth, while his younger brother Thomas also fought for Parliament, on one occasion being left for dead on the battlefield. But he lived to become a famous London doctor. Captain Francis Sydenham, later promoted to Major, was killed in 1645 during the defence of Chapel Fort, Weymouth.

In 1644 the Governor of Poole, John Bingham, wrote to the Lieutenant Governor of the Isle of Wight begging for reinforcements. He was afraid the town might not be able to beat off an attack by the 'malignants'. "We expect a falinge on by them every night ... On Saturday last there were landed 10 great flatt bottomed boates sent from Weymouth and brought to Corfe Castle which they kepe extreme private," wrote Bingham. Whether reinforcements came or not the Poole parliamentarians continued to meet with success. A Poole privateer captured two Royalist ships in Swanage Bay with a cargo of ammunition and cloth. Some of this was divided amongst the soldiers and sailors while the rest went to the citizens of Poole. But in spite of local successes the overall picture in Wessex was of Royalists triumphant and these were anxious days for Poole until the decisive battles of Marston Moor and Naseby in 1644 and 1645.

The hostilities in Dorset look to us today like a sort of war in miniature: four small boats working their way laboriously by sail and oar along the devious channels and winding river to attack Wareham with muskets: a few dozen infantrymen coming face to face with an enemy patrol beside a rustic bridge over the diminutive river Frome near Dorchester and the two sides bashing at each other until one or the other ran away.

Political upheavals were reflected in religious practice. In 1647 the vicar of St James, the Revd John Haddesley, was imprisoned by order of Oliver Cromwell. He was to be succeeded by a Mr Gardiner and this nomination aroused a storm of protest among the parishioners. Gardiner was a supporter of the most radical sects of the time: the Levellers, Ranters, Dippers are those mentioned by his opponents in Poole. The Quakers too were an important dissenting group and their founder, George Fox, visited Poole several times between 1655 and 1663. It was there that he converted William Bayly who became a devoted disciple and assistant. Bayly was imprisoned and later sentenced to be exiled to the West Indies but died on the outward voyage in 1675. He published thirty-five tracts or booklets, the last of which was entitled "A Testimony Against Drunkenness and Swearing".

The Mayor, William Williams, sided with the anti-Gardiner faction, and the military governor, Colonel J.Rede, gave way to their demands. However Rede himself was extremely unpopular, unlike his predecessor Colonel Bingham, and in 1651 the Mayor and Burgesses sent a petition to the Council of State asking for Rede to be removed. They complained that "he has laid upon us an insupportable burden of grief, for we see the members of Christ slighted and contemned; our civil rights devoured by the power of his arbitrary sword ..." The dispute dragged on indecisively, Major George Skurr failing to replace Rede. It appears that in the end a burgess named Burghogge was appointed officer in charge of the garrison.

In spite of Poole having been in the post-Civil War period a place where "famine and plague contend"- the phrase was used by Sir Anthony Ashley Cooper - the town continued to grow in strength. It was customary to assert its individuality in the old ceremony known as "Beating the Bounds". This dates from 1364 when a document known as the Winchelsea Certificate confirmed boundaries which had been defined in 1342. During the 17th century the 'perambulation' round the county borders, during which the proclamation of Poole's rights and limits is read out, took place at intervals and was sometimes put on record. In 1631 the ceremonies ended with a religious service. But later the event seems to have evolved towards the present-day style of a mixture of ceremony and entertainment. The account of 1649 mentions that the young men played "football with their hatts" while in 1667 it appears that the aldermen and burgesses indulged in "some merry pastime". Young men and women danced while "divers other men sported themselves at a play called hop-frog". The same spirit evidently enlivened the Purbeck quarrymen who kicked a football all the way from Corfe to Ower Quay when they visited the landlord to pay their rent.

The boundaries so defined extended to Bromehill, near Hamworthy, and westwards up the Wareham Channel to a point opposite Holton Mere formerly known as Shag Rock, where there was a stone. To the south the harbour limit was decided by dropping a barrel into the sea while observers on Sandbanks noted how far out it was when they could still just see it. The distance was about three miles, which leads to two conclusions: it was a very big barrel and the boundary ended at Handfast Point (Old Harry Rocks). As to distances to the north and east, they are lost in the sea mists of history.

From 1834 the custom of Beating the Bounds lapsed until it was revived in 1921 by Councillor Warne Julyan. It is now performed every three years. It has become one of those ancient ceremonies which have lost their practical value and which are kept up and elaborated for the sake of the spectacle and entertainment. Today boatloads of local lads dress up as pirates and engage in mock battles with water as the ammunition. An ever-growing flotilla of motor-boats processes round the familiar waterways, led by the Mayor and other civic dignitaries, who go ashore at the historic boundary marks.

After the victory of Cromwell, Charles II had to be off on what he referred to as his 'travels', and many are the hiding places where he is supposed to have spent a night or two. What is less often recounted is that he escaped to France on a Poole-based ship which was engaged on a regular run between Poole and Shoreham. This little collier was called the *Surprise* and it was at Shoreham that the King boarded it. He and Lord

Wilmot persuaded the captain, N.Tattershall, and crew to take them across the Channel. First they pretended to be setting off on the normal run to Poole, then turned south near the Isle of Wight, eventually landing at Fecamp. A northerly wind gave them an easy passage; and equally providentially the wind swung right round the compass to take the *Surprise* back to Poole.

Charles had promised Tattershall some reward, and when the ex-King was again on the throne he kept his promise. He awarded Captain Tattershall a pension of £100 a year, changed the name of the *Surprise* to *Royal Escape*, had her refitted and created her a ship of the Royal Navy, 'fifth-rate'.

The Restoration was greeted with general rejoicing, but there were many for whom it proved to be a disaster. The Clarendon Code was designed to suppress all the 'fringe' Christian movements, to which the parishioners of Poole themselves had objected, only to find themselves now forced towards the opposite extreme. A Commission was appointed to see that the civic officials and the clergy of Poole conformed with the Code. Its members included several burgesses non-resident in Poole who had been conspicuous supporters of the King. One of them was Captain Winston Churchill, one of whose twelve children, John Churchill, first Duke of Marlborough, became the most successful general in our history, and was ancestor of the 1940 wartime Prime Minister.

The Commission sat in Poole in 1662 and twenty-two burgesses refused to take the oath of conformity and submission, thus sacrificing their official positions. The Mayor was among them. Among the clergy who suffered was Samuel Hardy, the popular vicar of St James. The Royalists hated him but found him difficult to get rid of as Poole was what is known as a "Royal Peculiar" and to some extent independent of the ecclesiastical courts. However, the Commission secured his dismissal on the grounds that he did not observe all the details of approved ritual. For example, he did not wear a surplice or make the sign of the cross at baptism.

In September 1665 Charles II visited Poole. He had left London to get away from the Great Plague. In the ravaged capital the distraught citizens were resorting to such desperate measures as holding a tender young puppy against their pustules and firing muskets out of windows to kill germs, but occasionally striking down a neighbour quicker than the plague would have done. "Divers knights and squires and gentlemen of the county of Dorset and elsewhere came to wait upon his Majesty." The King's retinue included his illegitimate son the Duke of Monmouth, aged sixteen, the Earls of Suffolk, Oxford and Lauderdale, and the Lords Gerrard, Ashley, Crofts and Arlington. On that day everybody but the most dedicated must have been a Royalist. Two banquets were held, both in private houses, one being the home of Colonel William Skutt, whose father had been in charge of the Roundhead garrison in Poole. The Corporation Record Book refers to the visit as an "unparalleled honour" and to his "sacred royal presence". But the burgesses were practical as well as diplomatic: they took the opportunity to raise the question of Poole's special rights under its ancient Charters, which Charles had revoked. These were soon restored and some new concessions added.

After luncheon, the merry Monarch went on a trip to Brownsea Island, "rowed by six masters of shipps" in a boat owned by Colonel William Skutt; and the King brought his visit to a happy end by nominating Skutt as the next Mayor of Poole. But again the burgesses refused to be carried away on a tide of euphoric royalism. If they allowed the King to appoint the Mayor it would set a dangerous precedent and undermine their own powers of appointment. They therefore ignored the Monarch's request and handed the office of Mayor to Stephen Street.

Banquets and fine speeches were all very well, but the persecutions went on. So violent was the reaction that Oliver Cromwell's body was dug up and hanged at Tyburn. In July 1667 Samuel Pepys wrote: "Everybody do nowadays reflect upon Oliver and commend him, what brave things he did ... " It is in the records of Bristol Baptists that they were soon looking back to the Cromwellian era as "halcyon days of liberty, prosperity and peace". Poole's numerous nonconformists would no doubt have agreed with this. Cromwell had only persecuted the old Church of England and the Catholics. He allowed the Jews to return to England for the first time since 1290, when Edward I expelled them.

The Five Mile Act forbade the unorthodox to come within that range of a corporate town or to teach in schools. One of those so proscribed was the Revd John Wesley, grandfather of the founder of Methodism. He used to enter Poole secretly to preach to his followers and was imprisoned several times.

James II came to the throne in 1685 and proceeded to enforce pro-Catholic measures even more vigorously than Charles had done. Leading Whigs and Tories decided that they would be better served by William of Orange, who had been the heroic defender of Holland against the French. Support for James melted away and William was accepted by the Scots as well as the English. A small contribution which the citizens of Poole made to his success was to lure the captain of a fireship named *Speedwell* into the Antelope Hotel and detain him there while they appropriated his ship.

The nonconformist sects were now free to flourish and they certainly did so in Poole, though not without some quarrelling among themselves. One sign of this revival was the building of the Meeting House in Hill Street. A sect called the Arians caused Poole Congregationalists a good deal of trouble and gained control of the chapel which the latter had built in 1704. Much of the trouble revolved around the question of baptism and how it should be performed - whether the water should be sprinkled or used as a bath, and at what age the ceremony should be carried out.

Meanwhile England's newly-acquired Dutch King had dragged this country into a war with the French; and in 1690 Admiral Tourville brought a hundred ships to within a few miles of Poole. But he passed on and sacked Teignmouth instead. The following year he routed the British and

Dutch off Beachy Head, making the French masters of the Channel. The British fleet was overstretched and French privateers were able to inflict damaging losses on our merchant vessels. Among them were those of the Poole fishing fleet, whose main business was on the Newfoundland run, then back to the Mediterranean.

France and England were each preparing to invade the other. The British proposed to ferry an army across in 1,500 metal landing craft. At Cherbourg, the nearest point to Poole, 4,000 men were assembled. Admiral Tourville was ordered to convoy this force across the Channel but fared no better than Philip of Spain, Napoleon or Hitler. His fleet was scattered and slightly damaged off Barfleur and La Hogue in 1692. But the next year Tourville sank about a hundred British merchant vessels as they were returning richly laden from the Eastern Mediterranean. Then again the fortunes of war swung the other way when Admiral Rooke in a race to the English Channel got there ahead of Tourville and so thwarted Louis XIV's plans for invasion.

Against this background, Poole's Mayor, Henry Jubber, instituted an anti-invasion watch both at Poole and on Brownsea Island - that most strategically placed nature reserve in the mouth of the harbour. Also "four great guns" were to be mounted at the town gates and all small arms to be pooled at the Town Hall for servicing and distribution if needed. No wonder King William was pleased when in 1694 Captain Peter Joliffe rescued a fishing boat from a French privateer. His Majesty presented the Captain with a medal on a gold chain in recognition of his skill and boldness in "chaceing the said privateer on shoar near Lulworth on ye isle of Purbeck where shee was broken in peeces in 1694". Later, in the reign of George I, Captain Joliffe was given charge of all Poole's defences.

Another gold medallist was William Thomson who likewise succeeded in bringing home a French pirate which attacked his fishing boat. Our fishing vessels were lightly armed in those stirring times.

Meanwhile English landowners were paying £5 million a year in taxes, merchants were suffering severe losses and neither side could see much prospect of an early victory. Peace talks therefore began and merchants and seamen alike thanked God. But there was another enemy continually eroding the profits of British businessmen and manufacturers - the smugglers. Smuggling was so widespread and well-organised that Poole councillors petitioned Prime Minister Walpole to take action. His response was so vigorous that the councillors and everyone else were soon wishing they had kept quiet. The trading community were imprisoned and fined by the dozen, often unaware of the fact that they had been dealing in smuggled goods. Many of the victims were sea captains whose confinement caused serious losses to Poole's seaborne trade.

Robert Walpole wanted to extend the Excise system to wine and tobacco. These goods would then be transferred from ship to warehouse and taxed thereafter. This system meant tight control, whereas customs officers were easily evaded. But Parliament threw out Walpole's Bill. In spite of the fact that it would have eased the burden of taxation on the landed gentry their Members of Parliament looked with such horror on any further encroachment of government controls, they were incapable of seeing reason. What Parliament did instead was to enact more punitive laws against smugglers. Under one of these a man could be hanged for blacking his face, a common practice among smugglers working at night.

Between 1723 and 1733, 192,515 gallons of brandy and 1,061,268 pounds of tobacco were seized by customs officers; and this was believed to amount to only one-tenth of the total of these goods illegally imported. Tobacco was commonly on sale at prices which would have been unprofitable had duty been paid. As the population of England, Scotland and Wales at this time is supposed to have been around ten millions, there was a pound of smuggled tobacco for every man, woman and child in the United Kingdom. The Prime Minister himself, like other country gentlemen, had at one time dealt in smuggled goods.

It was natural enough that the national hobby should flourish along the wild coasts of Devon, Dorset and Hampshire, including the quiet backwaters of Poole Harbour. There was no town at Bournemouth, and there too on that open sandy beach illicit cargoes were landed and rustled inland to hiding places on the moors and in the New Forest.

Dramatic episodes in the story of smuggling have been so often recorded that it would be superfluous to recount more than a few of them here. One of the most unusual glimpses into the reality of that underworld comes to us through the Memoirs of the third Earl of Malmesbury, who recalled an incident reminiscent of the opening scene of *Great Expectations*. In about the year 1800 he was bird-nesting as a small boy in the area between Bournemouth and Christchurch "when a rough fellow seized me and seeing I was frightened was very civil, promising to let me go if I did not resist. He kept his word and made me swear I would not tell ... I did not betray the man or his companions, whom I saw in the woods hiding kegs of brandy, of which they insisted on giving me a specimen".

A smuggler whose name is remembered locally is Isaac Gulliver, who successfully evaded the Revenue officers throughout his life and died at Wimborne in 1822. His house there bears the nameplate 'Gulliver House'. Previously he had been in the wines and spirits business at Kinson. In 1782 the Government offered to pardon smugglers who gave themselves up if they would then serve in the Navy. This could also be done by proxy if the accused could find a volunteer. Gulliver availed himself of this facility. He is believed to have master-minded a network stretching from Poole to Dover. Possibly the by-way called Gulliver's Close at Lilliput, two miles from Poole, gets its name from him rather than from Swift's giant.

Gulliver bribed someone to serve in the Navy for him and likewise left the nastier side of smuggling to others. Not so an earlier exponent of the business named Kingsmill who led a group called the Hawkhurst Gang. A member of this gang named Perin was sailing home from Guernsey with a cargo of tea and liquor when the ship was boarded by Revenue officers and the cargo confiscated and stored in the Customs House at Poole. The tea alone was worth £500, a fortune in those days, and the smugglers bitterly resented its loss. Sixty of them decided to raid the Customs House and retrieve their loot, and this they did on 6 October 1747. They smashed their way into the building, seized 37 hundredweight of tea and set off for Fordingbridge with their well-laden train of horses. Of course many people must have seen them, but those who did would either be sympathisers or too frightened to talk. There were, however, two exceptions, a cobbler named Chater and an elderly man named Galley. These two decided to inform a JP at Chichester of Kingsmill's activities: the gang's network, it seems, extended into Sussex. But news of the informers' intent leaked out. On the way to Chichester the old man and the cobbler were set upon by members of the gang, tortured and murdered.

The trial took place in April 1748. Those accused of breaking into the Customs House were tried at the Old Bailey. Three out of five were hanged.

But smuggling was seldom so dramatic or violent. In Poole, a considerable traffic was carried on by means of some large drains which ran from the Quay to the streets behind, as if placed especially for the convenience of smugglers. One of these drains connected with an inn of those days called the Baker's Arms. When flood water coursed down a drain a log could be tied to a rope and sent on its way to the Quay for attachment to its precious burden.

Evidence that smuggling was a paying game may be seen in the fines imposed in 1816 on Joseph Brooks and Martha Hurdle for "harbouring and concealing" a quantity of silk shawls, handkerchiefs, gloves and 40 yards of lace. She was fined £20 and Brooks £10.6s. In the same year John Galton and Timothy Ellis paid a worse penalty when they were caught smuggling at Studland: they were 'impressed' into the Navy.

The Revenue men of those days were regarded very much as the Inland Revenue is today - a faceless bureaucracy whom it was no crime to out-manoeuvre. "I like a smuggler," wrote Charles Lamb. "He is the only honest thief. He robs nothing but the Revenue, an abstraction I never greatly cared about. Adam Smith, who was not only an economist but a Commissioner of Customs, said that a smuggler was a "respectable person" and the victim of a silly law. He was guilty of a "crime which nature never meant to be so". Even the Revd James Woodforde accepted smuggled goods without a qualm: "Andrews the smuggler brought me ...a bag of Hyson tea 6lb in weight. He frightened us a little by whistling under the parlour window just as we were going to bed. I gave him some Geneva [gin] and paid him for the tea at 10/6 per pound."

Smuggling enriched a few and provided relatively cheap goods for many more. But Poole was now building up an honest and highly profitable trade based on the enterprise of its fishing fleet. It was the period during which the Newfoundland cod fisheries brought Poole its era of greatest prosperity.

It all started with an idea in the mind of King Henry VII in the late fifteenth century. He thought that if a route to the east could be found by sailing west, English merchant ships would be able to avoid the Venetians, who controlled the established trade routes. Henry narrowly missed sponsoring Columbus and then in 1469 he invited John Cabot to sail "all parts, regions and coasts of the eastern, western and northern sea". So Newfoundland was discovered.

It is usually quoted as a good joke that Henry VII paid Cabot £10 for his discovery. But that is only part of the story. The famous navigator also received not only a pension of £20 a year, but was granted ownership and a trading monopoly of the lands he discovered provided that the King received 20 percent of the profits.

The Guildhall, built in 1761 — the first year of George III's long reign — drawn by Sheila Sturdy in 1949. It is seen from Market Street with a Georgian backdrop that was bulldozed in the 1960s.

FORTUNES from FISH

NOBODY COULD fail to notice that the Banks, off Newfoundland, were teeming with cod. One observer said you could let down a basket and haul it up full of fish. Within a few years fishing vessels from the south of England were making regular voyages across the Atlantic to the fishing grounds.

Newfoundland was formally proclaimed a colony in 1583 when twenty British ships were in St John's Harbour. The enterprising gentleman who performed this ceremony was Sir Humphrey Gilbert, who had often been at Poole and who was responsible for declaring the number of armed men available at the time of the Armada. When he applied for a 'patent' to found a colony in North America, he put it to the Privy Council that his proposed expedition to that part of the world and to the West Indies would "annoye the King of Spayne" and damage the Queen's enemies, or as he put it, "pare their nayles to the stumpes".

The fishing industry based on Newfoundland did not grow in a steady progression. It fluctuated widely, so that while in 1591 it is recorded that forty-six ships were on the Newfoundland run from Poole, in 1627 the Mayor complained that he could only muster sixteen. The fishing fleet was subjected intermittently throughout the sixteenth and seventeenth centuries to damaging attacks by the warships of France and by pirates not only from that country but also from Turkey and North Africa.

The sixteenth century situation in which the English buccaneers had preyed at will on French and Spanish merchantmen was now reversed. Several times the Mayors of Poole, Dartmouth and other West Country ports begged the King and Parliament for protection. On one of these occasions the answer they received was that they had better "forbear their trade". Sometimes merchants engaged their own privateers to protect their vessels. There were simply not enough warships to go round: the Navy was overstretched.

In 1618 the merchants of several seaports, including Poole, sent a petition to James I referring to the "infinite spoyles done of late to his subjects by pyratts". In the last few years they had lost "300 sayle of ships to the utter ruine of themselves and impoverishment of the realm".

However, James did help by appointing as chief protector of British merchant vessels and pirate-hunter Sir John Mainwaring, who had himself been a pirate. Among his feats were the rescue of the Newfoundland fishing fleet from a Barbary pirate and the capture of two Turkish pirate ships in the Thames Estuary. A North African pirate actually reached Poole and in 1638 the *Concord* of Poole fought a three-hour bloody battle with a

Turkish pirate, drove it off and brought back to Poole one Turkish prisoner and three rescued Christians. The Poole boat was owned by Thomas Robarts, several times Lord Mayor, and the captain was Mr Nurrey.

In 1665 the Dutch burned St John's, even then a centre of British trade. The French attacked English settlements in 1697, 1705 and 1708. Again during the American War of Independence the coast of Newfoundland was ravaged and the fishing trade damaged. With the Seven Years' War and the Napoleonic Wars as well, the transatlantic fisheries certainly had to battle against appalling odds. In 1797 for example, the *General Wolfe* from Poole was seized by a French privateer on the way to Newfoundland. However on this occasion the fishing vessel succeeded in throwing off its attacker. In 1702 a letter from Poole mentions a French warship having captured seven English ships off the Newfoundland coast.

As if it were not enough to be plundered by the French and the Turks, our fishermen also had to contend with the press gangs, not only on land but at sea. Warships frequently accosted merchant vessels and took away as many men as they dared. However, it seems there were limits. In 1759 a Captain Fortescue was fined £1,000 and costs for seizing so many men off a Poole fishing boat that the vessel was helpless and foundered. In 1794 the merchant ship *Maria* was approached in Studland Bay by a vessel carrying a press gang and a body of soldiers. The *Maria* tried to escape and was fired on and five people were killed. We know that in 1672 one hundred and fifty Poole men were pressed into Naval service, some dragged from their homes.

This system of random enforced service was hated by everyone from the Mayor downwards. As soon as news filtered through that the King or Parliament had ordered a number of men to be pressed into service from Poole, there was a rush for the exits. Likely lads went almost literally underground in disused quarries in the Purbeck Hills. Fishing captains hoisted sail and headed post haste for Newfoundland - which is why the Navy had to chase them on the high seas. Both Poole and Weymouth received formal complaints from the Admiralty Commissioners about this unpatriotic behaviour. It was after all illogical for merchants to complain about the depredations of pirates and then refuse to contribute men for the Navy. The men of Poole always thought that others were better able than they to meet the demands of their rulers, especially when it came to supplying ships. In 1592 the Privy Council had protested to the Mayor of Poole that Poole sea captains, when told they must give up their vessels "did unfurnish theire shippes and used verie lewd and undutifulle speeches". Perhaps the most distasteful duty the Mayor had to carry out in those times was to sign the document authorising a press gang to seize a number of men.

A vivid picture of life on both sides of the water has come to us through Edmund Gosse, the distinguished biographer and man of letters of Victorian times. He was the son of Philip Henry Gosse, who was brought to live in Poole when he was two years old and became a well-known biologist.

In 1825, when he was fifteen, Philip went to work as a junior clerk in the offices of George Garland, near Poole Quay. The Garlands were one of the most successful merchants and shipowners in the Poole-Newfoundland fisheries, and although the trade was by this time in decline, it was still very substantial. "The counting house was a spacious, old-fashioned apartment, adapted from a sort of corridor in the rambling family mansion ... A portentous hush broken only by the squeaking of pens was accustomed to reign in that solemn apartment." But "the time he spent in Mr Garland's office was very pleasant".

Recording his father's reminiscences, Edmund Gosse writes: "The Borough and County of Poole, to give it its full honours, possessed in those days a population of about six thousand souls. It was a prosperous little town whose good streets ... were lined with solid and comfortable red brick houses. The upper part of the Borough was clean, the sandy soil on which it was built aiding a rapid drainage after rain. The lower streets, such as the sea end of Lagland and Fish Streets, the Strand and the lanes abutting on the Quay, were filthy enough; while the nose was certainly not regaled by the reeking odours of the Quay itself, with its stores and piles of salt cod, its ranges of barrels of train oil, its rope and tar and turpentine, and its well-stocked shambles for fresh fish, sometimes too obviously in the act of becoming stale fish. Yet among seaport towns its character was one of exceptional sweetness and cleanliness. And here, though the memory is of some years later, I may print my father's impression of the Poole of his early childhood (about 1820)":

"The Quay with its shipping and sailors: their songs and cries of 'Heave with a will yo-ho'; the busy merchants bustling to and fro: fishermen and boatmen and hoymen in their sou'westers, Guernsey frocks and loose trousers; countrymen, young bumpkins in smocks seeking to be shipped as youngsters for Newfoundland; rows of casks redolent of train oil; Dobell the ganger moving among them, rod in hand; Customs officers and tide-waiters taking notes; piles of salt fish loading; packages of dry goods being shipped; coal cargoes discharging; dogs in scores; idle boys larking about or mounting the rigging; all this makes a lively picture in my memory, while the church bells, a full peal of eight, are ringing merrily. The Poole men gloried somewhat in the peal; and one of the low inns frequented by sailors in one of the lanes opening on the Quay had for its sign the Eight Bells duly depicted in full.

"Owing to the narrow, winding channels of Poole Harbour, skilled pilots were indispensible for every vessel arriving or sailing. From our upper windows in Skinner Street we could see the vessels pursuing their course along the Main Channel, now approaching Lilliput, then turning and apparently coasting under the Sandbanks at North Haven Point. Pilots, fishermen, boatmen, a loosely-trousered, Guernsey-frocked sou'-westered race, were always lounging about the Quay."

On the Newfoundland side it was very different and a complete contrast to the "warmth and comfort and congenial company of the counting house. The dirty brawling vulgar fellows ... uttering their low, witless jokes ... cursing, swearing, abusing others ... filth everywhere, rancid grease."

Philip Henry Gosse went to Newfoundland in 1827 and the next year "I was sent to the oil-storage to take count of the seal pelts delivered. The stage was a long projecting wharf, roofed and enclosed, carried out over the sea on piles ... I take my place, paper and pencil in hand ... seated on an inverted tub ... A boat, loaded to the water's edge with seal pelts is being slowly pulled from one of the schooners by a noisy crew, mostly Irish. "Some of the crew throw the heavy pelts of greasy, bloody fat upon the floor of the stage. The rancid grease could not fail to be absorbed by my shoes and scattered over my clothes; so that whenever at bell-ringing or in the evening I essayed to join my companions, the plain-spoken rogues would welcome me with: 'Oh Gosse, pray don't come very near! You stink so of sea-oil!' Then at times the bitter cold of winter, the snowy gales driving in on me and blowing up through the corduroy poles which made the floor: all this made me heartily glad when the last schooner was discharged ..."

Naturalist and nature-lover Philip Gosse also writes of his interest in the life of the seals, and of the seal-hunters. He must have been horrified at the hunting of young seals with "gaffs and guns, others pelting them and others dragging their loads of pelts to their boats".

At its peak in the late eighteenth and early nineteenth centuries, the Poole-Newfoundland fishing fleet numbered between three and four hundred vessels. Coincidentally it was a period of nationwide affluence in Britain. The contemporary historian William Hewitt wrote: "The tables of mechanics were heaped with loads of viands of the best quality ... their houses were full of furniture - clocks, tables, looking-glasses and prints stuck on every possible space on the walls, and from the ceilings depending hams, baskets, bags, fly-cages of many colours that gave their abodes more the aspect of ware-rooms or museums rather than dwellings of the working class."

If he succeeded in joining the crew of a fishing boat, the green Dorset villager would find himself racing across the Atlantic on the First of March in an event which had become a sort of annual regatta. The fishing captains crowded on sail to the point of danger, racing to secure the best berths on the other side. In the foregoing centuries the first arrival also put himself in charge of affairs in Newfoundland, where a handful of settlers often wrecked the fishermen's huts in their absence. The "fishing admirals" were replaced by a naval commander in 1729.

"When fogs are thick and nights are dark ice-floes threaten much peril, yet on runs the ship amain," says one writer. The Dutch head of state, De Witt, expressed the opinion that "the English Navy first became formidable by the discovery of the rich fishery of Newfoundland".

Having been almost frightened and frozen to death and fed on almost uneatable food, the country lad at sea would then have to begin to learn the craft of cod-fishing. It was done from small boats using hand-lines with hundreds of hooks on each line. Each hook had to be baited from a supply of stinking fish refuse. When it came to pay, the recruit would find that he was paid according to what was known as the "Trucking system", which obliged him to obtain goods from his employer. When he eventually got back to Poole he might even find that he owed money instead of having some in his pocket.

According to F.W.Mathews, whose study of the Poole-Newfoundland trade is probably the most thorough yet made, each ship caught an average of 50,000 fish in a season and also brought back several tons of what they called "train oil". How strange that the chroniclers of these events invariably leave the reader to guess the meaning of this misleading term. It comes from the old German 'Trane', meaning a tear or drop of other extruded liquid. To the fisherman it simply meant fish-liver oil. For centuries in northern Europe it had been used as a lamp oil, for treating leather, and as a medicine. The Scots of the Western Isles knew it as a remedy for rickets and bone ailments. In 1563 the traveller Samuel Purchas wrote that the Icelanders "plucke out the bones and lay out their bowels and make fat or Oyle out of them". A typical food of the strong-stomached Icelanders was a mixture of mutton tallow and fish-liver.

The simplest way of obtaining the oil was to put the livers in a barrel and wait for them to decay, when the oil rose to the surface. The records of the Poole trade refer to 'pressing', while more advanced methods involve heating. But no matter how it was extracted, the smell of 'train oil' was so repugnant that is was unpopular even for use in lamps.

In 1782 orthodox medicine caught up with folk wisdom when Dr Kay and Dr Darbey of Manchester Infirmary discovered that cod oil was good for certain afflictions of the joints. The doctors reported that many patients were unable to take the new remedy because of its nauseating smell, but so impressed were they with the results that they ordered sixty gallons a year. It was not until a hundred years later that the word 'vitamin' began to enter the language. Strangely, cod liver is nowhere near so rich in vitamins A and D as the liver of many other fish, including the bass, halibut and tunny. But there was plenty of it available.

The following extract from *The Diary of a Country Parson* by Revd James Woodforde shows that the use of cod liver oil was widespread before its official recognition, as the Diary was written in Oxford and Somerset between 1758 and 1781: "Mr Thorne sent Nancy over to day some Cod's Liver Oil to make use of about her stiff arm and lame knee. Pray God! send thy blessing upon it for her good."

High Street, Poole, in 1870. The engraving, by Newman and Company, shows the town stepping out into Victorian prosperity. The Post Office was built on the corner with Hill Street.

POTTERY and PUBS

ARTHUR BRYANT has called his study of the late eighteenth and early nineteenth centuries *The Age of Elegance*. Another writer once dubbed it "The Era of Dirty Lace". It is an apt comment on a time when there were unwashed bodies beneath the frills, and piles of filth in the streets. Beyond the walls of the country estates and the stately mansions there were areas of extreme poverty in both town and country. Children could still be hanged for stealing and there were a hundred other offences for which the penalty was death. Not surprisingly, it was seldom carried out and hangings were certainly not common in Poole. There are, however, records of murderers being burnt on the hand and beggars were still occasionally whipped.

Worse than these punishments was the appallingly unhealthy condition of the majority of prisons in England. The Corporation records contain frequent complaints that the prisons are insecure and in 1805 reference is also made to the lack of comfort for the inmates. Such a complaint could hardly have been made, however, about the Fish Street prison in 1777 when the Keeper, John Galton, was given a month's notice for "suffering it to be used as a common bawdy house".

The trouble was the lack of sanitation, They did not like the filth, but they just could not think what to do about it. The problem grew as the urban population grew. As far back as 1610 a scavenger was appointed to remove all "soil, compost and dung" and everybody had to contribute to his pay. In 1844 no fewer than fifty-three overflowing cesspits were found under Windsor Castle. The drains were made of wood and leaked, but only a few doctors ever suspected a connection between the drains and the frequent deaths of men and women, young and old, from 'fever'.

When the truth was discovered, Poole's pottery industry was to benefit from the introduction of earthenware drainpipes. Looking back to 1837 when her mother died of 'fever' Lady Georgina Russell remarks in her memoirs that "in those careless days no one thought of bad drains, indeed bad drains were considered rather a joke. If they smelt, people considered it a sign of bad weather approaching and were rather pleased to have the warning."

The water-closet had begun to make its appearance in the previous century, but even in the 1830s these would only be found in the houses of the well-to-do. Poorer people used an earth closet or had a privy set over a cesspit. Baths with running water were equally uncommon. Celia Fiennes, who described the extraction of alum and iron sulphate from the deposits on Brownsea Island in 1682, in 1700 visited Chatsworth, the seat of the

Duke of Devonshire, and gazed in wonder at "a batheing room fitted with two locks to let in one hott, the other cold water to attemper it as persons please". It would still have been a rarity a century later and the Duke of Wellington was considered eccentric because he took a bath daily. In 1812 the Lord Mayor of London asked if he might have a shower installed in his residence, but the Common Council refused. Other Lord Mayors had managed well enough without a shower, hadn't they? "In the days of the Georges," writes Mrs C.S.Peel, "it was not unfashionable to be dirty."

The practice of hygiene and waste disposal had scarcely changed since the Middle Ages, but even with this knowledge one can only feel some amazement on seeing the frequency of complaints about the dumping of rubbish and sewage recorded in the minutes of the Poole Quarter Sessions during this period. Between 1810 and 1817 the reprimands and fines for leaving filth around and obstructing the streets run into dozens. The scavengers are in continual trouble for not doing their unpleasant work properly. On one occasion they are reproved for leaving "large heaps of dirt in every street in the town", while on another they have failed to put up rails at the end of Hosier's Lane to prevent people from falling into the Common Sewer.

This must have been a trench into which tributary drains ran from every street and in which refuse could be dumped. In an effort to keep the filth moving, two Surveyors in 1832 made an "earnest request that every householder will cause six buckets of water (at the least) to be thrown into the gutter opposite his house every morning at nine o'clock, to keep the streets clean and wholesome". In 1828 a Mrs Fisher is 'presented' at the Quarter Sessions for allowing "offensive and pernicious smells" to emanate from her premises in Thames Street. Another lady was in trouble for depositing soot near the road and somebody else in 1822 caused an obstruction on the Quay by leaving some cannon there where they accumulated "filth and dirt". "Insufferable smells" are often mentioned and evidently people were not insensitive to dirt, just as they were not unaware of the inhumanity of life in prison. But they still had to invent ways of coping with these problems.

Pigs feature frequently in the Quarter Sessions records. People kept them here, there and everywhere, and often they got loose and wandered or were kept in places where they caused inconvenience. Horses could also cause trouble, and drivers are reprimanded for their habit of walking ahead of the horses, "who gallop after them whereby accidents happen to children and passengers ... a growing Evil".

An offence even more common than leaving rubbish about was selling short measure. So numerous are the fines imposed for these minor frauds on the customer, one can only conclude that the average shopkeeper or stall-holder had pretty low standards of honesty. One may feel some surprise that in those days of unfettered free enterprise the Corporation and the law exercised such a degree of protection and regulation. The poor were not forgotten. There were the Alms Houses, and on special occasions, special gifts. In 1809 there were found to be six hundred and forty-seven families deserving of charity to celebrate the jubilee of King Gerorge III. This share-out included seven bullocks, six sheep and two thousand loaves.

Before leaving the criminal records, it may be worth noting that in 1835 people were still being sent to America or Australia as a punishment for felony.

The frequent trouble caused by pigs running loose in the streets has already been mentioned, and they were only a part of the livestock kept within the town boundaries. When estimating the country's preparedness against invasion by Napoleon, the Government found that Poole could muster twenty-three cows, one hundred and ninety-nine pigs and three sheep. Presumably the inspectors did not think the hens worth counting, though many a cottager must have cherished one or two. Surely there must also have been a few goats grazing on the rough land outside the town boundaries. The population of Poole at this time is estimated to have been about six thousand.

However invasion never came, and in 1814 it was time to celebrate the victory over Napoleon. The cost to Poole of these festivities was £463.2s.6d., a budget in which priority was given to "strong beer", of which the merry fishermen and chandlers and merchants drank 1,280 gallons, value £96. Poole's breweries had been an important local industry at least since the 16th century, when licences were issued to "kepe a common alehouse or Typlynge House".

If there was one section of the British people who had little cause to join in the celebrations of 1814 it was the soldiers who had won the war and conquered a new empire. Their barrack rooms were grossly overcrowded, sanitary arrangements were disgustingly primitive, and they were given two meals a day at 7.30 a.m. and 12.30 p.m. consisting of beef which could only be boiled, because the only cooking utensil was a pot. They drowned their woes in cheap poisonous liquor and their death-rate was fifteen per thousand at home, seventy-one per thousand in Jamaica and seventy to eighty in West Africa. They sweltered and died from malaria and too much salt beef. If they rebelled they were flogged. It was not until 1836 that any attempt was made to improve the lot of the soldier through better food, shorter service abroad and less brutal punishment.

About the time of Waterloo the Corporation owned two breweries which it leased out to the brewers. The beer flowed out to a thirsty public through thirty or more pubs and taverns, including the Shipwright's Arms, the Jolly Sailor, the Dolphin, Portmahon Castle and the Royal Oak – all familiar names to us today. But beyond these sprang up numerous 'alehouses' where the customer could find not only beer, but also women. To run such a house was quite a common way for a widow to support herself, and several were prosecuted for doing so. So were prostitutes. In 1822 one Maria Williams was sentenced to one month in the "House of Correction" on the charge that "she did wander about in the public streets as a

Common Prostitute or Night Walker .. an idle and disorderly person".

In those two decades preceding the accession of Queen Victoria the British people were groping their way towards greater political democracy and seeking solutions to the new problems created by the Industrial Revolution. Politically it was a period of strife and unrest for Poole and Dorset. Farm labourers were so violently rebellious that in 1830 the Lord of the Manor of Canford raised a force to two hundred special constables as a precaution. Fortunately he did not have to use them.

In the commercial sphere Poole had lost more than 75 per cent of the great fish trade with Newfoundland. However, the contemporary commercial directories mention it as an important industry, supplied by the makers of ropes, sailcloth, clothing and other goods. One of the foremost names in the transatlantic fisheries was that of Spurrier. They built Upton House on the eastern side of the harbour and in the 1820s owned the biggest ship from Poole, the *Upton* of three hundred and twenty tons. Yet in 1830 the family went bankrupt, due to the decline of the Newfoundland trade combined with over-ambitious development of the Upton estate.

Other trades which flourished in Poole during this period were boot and shoe repairers numbering fifteen and bakers and flour dealers eighteen, while the corn trade was reported as being "very considerable". Grain was both exported and imported and there were good storage facilities on the Quay. Chandlery was of course an important business, especially as there were no fewer than fourteen ship and boat builders in Poole in these post-Waterloo decades. Every year about one hundred foreign vessels put in at Poole while the port was used by some eight hundred coastal traders, twelve of which plied between Poole and London. Commercial directories of the time report that "the oyster trade employs many boats and other fish are taken in the harbour in great numbers".

The oyster fishery was strictly controlled. Now many shipowners who had prospered in the Poole-Newfoundland fishery were desperate for business and they turned to Poole's native oysters. That the conservation laws were frequently broken is shown by the increasing number of prosecutions. The name of a certain Samuel Hart appears in 1821 and again in 1824 in connection with illegal oyster-dredging, the penalty for which could be a fine of forty shillings. On one occasion he was accused of dredging during the hours of darkness "contrary to the orders of the Mayor and Admiral".

Licences were granted to the oyster fishermen at the rate of about fifty a year. But in 1835 the Admiralty annulled the legal powers which Poole Corporation had formerly exercised over the harbour. Controls on fishing disappeared and so did the oysters. This considerable branch of the fishing industry had to wait until 1885 for a planned revival.

A dramatic new development took place in 1958 with the formation of Poole Oyster Company. This venture was founded by a few enterprising men who called themselves the Poole Technical Group. They owned one boat. After several changes of ownership the declining oyster industry was taken over by Messrs Fitch Lovell, of Smithfield, London. In 1973 the company began to breed Pacific oysters which mature in half the time it takes the European oyster to reach an acceptable size. The Pacific oyster can survive our average winter, but the Arctic conditions of 1962-63 were a testing time for it. However it survived and flourished, and the main problem was not to produce oysters but to market them. More Poole oysters, the manager reported in 1978, were eaten in Blackpool than in Poole. In the 1970s the company was also marketing clams, some of which came from Southampton and had to spend three weeks suspended from rafts in the harbour to cleanse them of hydrocarbon contamination – in plain English, to get rid of the effects of oil spillages.

Unfortunately the new company did not prosper, and Fitch Lovell sold their lease to Franklin's Fish Farms, a Dorset company. But progress was delayed because of fears about the effects of drilling for oil in the harbour. These fears were allayed by measures including a replanning of the oyster beds, and a renascence of the cultivation of the Pacific oyster was planned in 1986.

Once again overfishing threatened the native oyster, and in 1985 the Harbour Commissioners decided to issue no more licences for three years. However, those with unexpired licences continued to dredge the precious mollusc.

At the same time a disease which afflicts oysters had been noticed and one must hope that its damage will be limited. Some years ago Whitstable oysters were decimated by disease, and the once famous fleet of fishing boats is reduced to a single boat.

As if these natural hazards were not enough, a new danger appeared in the form of a man-made poison. This was the new and efficient anti-fouling tributyle tin (TBT) paint. Unfortunately the price of keeping ships' bottoms clear of weed and barnacles for months longer than was possible hitherto is that other forms of marine life suffer as well. There is little doubt that the larvae of the oyster suffer to some extent from this poison while it is also said to cause a thickening of the shell. The native 'flat' oyster is less susceptible to these effects than the Pacific variety. TBT anti-fouling is now banned.

Having survived for so many centuries it is unlikely that the oyster, either at Poole or elsewhere, will cease to exist; it seems equally unlikely that we shall ever regain the situation of a hundred years ago, when 310,000 barrels of oysters were consumed in London, let alone the carefree oyster-happy days of the middle ages, when eggs were six times as expensive as oysters. It was some compensation to Poole that at the time when the great days of transatlantic fishing were fast fading, another of its industries based on local resources was entering its greatest period.

The mining of ball clay, or pipe-clay as it used to be known, was already a cottage industry in pre-Roman times and there was a small pottery at Hamworthy before the Norman conquest. The claybeds are found on the low-lying heathlands of the Bagshot beds bordering the harbour and across to the slopes of the Purbeck Hills.

In the eighteenth and early nineteenth centuries the clay was dug by hand, loaded on to donkeys or wagons, and carried to various quays along the harbour coastline. There it was loaded on to barges, shipped to Poole and transferred to seagoing ships, often vessels which had been engaged in the Newfoundland fishery.

Three names dominated the industry at this stage: Thomas Hyde, Benjamin Fayle and the Pike Brothers. Thomas Hyde was born in 1731 and became a prominent figure in local business and politics. In 1770 he moved into the clay mining business and took up residence at Arne, where he paid £30 a year for the mining rights. His venture came to an end during a business recession in 1792, leaving as its memorial a small lake on the Arne peninsula and the name Hyde's Quay on the Wareham Channel.

Three years later Benjamin Fayle opened claypits near Corfe Castle and shipped his product from Middlebere Quay, a long finger of water opposite Round Island and pointing towards Corfe – so shallow now that only a dinghy can reach it even at high water.

The Pike brothers came from Devon and began mining in 1860 at Furzebrook, near Corfe. They shipped their clay from Wareham and later laid a light railway connecting it with Furzebrook. Rail transport had first arrived in Dorset with Fayle's horsedrawn tramway to Middlebere in 1805, and by 1906 the network of narrow gauge steam railways extended all across the Purbeck heaths from Povington to Goathorn. Some of the lines were still in use near Corfe after the last war. In the early days of the nineteenth century the wagons were drawn by horses. Meanwhile on the other side of the harbour the quays of Poole were being extended to meet the demands of increasing seaborne commerce.

The mining of clay kept pace with the growth of the Staffordshire Potteries and by 1820 the volume of clay being shipped out of Poole reached 20,000 tons a year. It is said that by 1840 35 per cent of all pottery produced in England was made from Poole clay. In 1859 it was 60,000 tons, but by 1910 it had fallen to 22,000.

While in the Midlands they were producing the artistic creations inspired by Josiah Wedgwood, Poole's local potteries were chiefly concerned with more mundane if essential objects such as drainpipes and bricks and tobacco pipes. However the Architectural Pottery Company, established at Hamworthy in 1859, produced mosaic and other decorative tiles. Besides this firm, *Kelly's Directory* of 1867 states that there were then "six large pottery works with a very large and lucrative trade". There were also several small firms making a living out of the local clay.

Carter's Poole Pottery as we know it today may be said to have been founded in 1873 by Jesse Carter, who revived a dying business and died in 1927 aged 97. He came from King's Worthy, near Winchester.

One of the most notable potteries was the South Western Pottery at Parkstone, founded by George Jennings in 1856. Like not a few other businessmen, one of his reasons for extending his business to Poole was his love for the East Dorset landscape. George Jennings was a man of considerable creative ability and enterprise. In the semi-rural Parkstone-Lilliput area he established a farm and a village, both now swallowed up in the spread of suburb and industry.

The age of steam came to the wild heathlands in the shape of two small railway engines called Tiny and Thames. They linked up various clay mines and one branch extended to the end of Goathorn Point. Until the Second World War wagonloads of Purbeck stone were being carried along this line to be tipped on to barges waiting below the pierhead. The huge blocks of stone were shot down a wooden chute, producing a noise that two miles away sounded like a not very distant thunderstorm. The barges, which must have been immensely strong to withstand such an impact, were then towed to the port side of the Swash Channel, opposite Studland Bay, and their load dumped to form the stone barrier called the Training Bank, the object of which was to confine the tidal stream and so deepen the channel, the main access route to Poole. These barges, normally used for dredging, have a bottom section divided down the middle and capable of being opened downwards so that the cargo simply drops through.

Poole clay went not only to the Midlands but to London, often carried from Poole in Henry Burden's ships. The Goathorn area was quite a busy little colony in Edwardian days. At the base of the headland were several cottages, a small school and a shed for the servicing of the railway engines. No 'Beeching Axe' was needed in 1970 when the little railway was torn up, after the many busy years of Tiny and Thames puffing their way across the heather and under the branches of the Goathorn woods.

Between 1920 and 1930 there was a sudden revival in the export of ball clay brought about by some half-dozen Italian schooners built in Denmark and acquired by Italy as a cheap form of sea transport. The *Willi Taaks* and the *Fratelli Garre* rubbed sides at Poole Quay and in 1933 with their graceful sister ships carried 35,000 tons of clay to Savona, Leghorn and Civitavecchia.

There followed a period of decline and in 1952 only 6,600 tons of clay were exported. But in the postwar period this trend has been dramatically reversed, until today more that 100,000 tons of clay are produced annually. The Pike Brothers and the Benjamin Fayle Company amalgamated in 1949 and were themselves taken over in 1968 by English China Clays (Ball Clays) Ltd., who now operate about twenty clay workings, both mines and open pits, based on the yards and processing works at Furzebrook.

The old method of open mining left scars on the landscape which turned into lakes or reverted to heath; the modern way is to go underground, in contrast to stone quarrying. English China Clays have extended their activities to the moors bordering the Wareham Channel, not far from where the Celts made pots for the Roman army – batches of them reached Hadrian's Wall – and where Thomas Hyde ventured into clay mining two hundred years ago. He would have been astonished to know that the views of nature conservationists carry considerable weight with regard to future plans and that these plans are conditioned by a small, odd-looking bird called the Dartford Warbler.

32 West Street, Poole, drawn in 1950. This imposing rusticated frontage, just north of Bay Hog Lane, has moulded architraves and keystones. Its centrepiece is an early nineteenth century flat-topped porch supported by Roman-Doric columns.

SIXTY GLORIOUS YEARS

THE BRITISH had put an end to absolute monarchy in 1688, but on the Continent of Europe that struggle had not been finally resolved. This fact was dramatically demonstrated to the people of Poole when the deposed King of France, Charles X, sailed into the port in 1830. On a warehouse near the King Charles Inn, there used to be a plaque inscribed: "King Charles X, dethroned King of France and his family landed at this quay on the 16th August 1830 from the English packet ship Great Britain." However, every other writer on the subject states that the King arrived on board the steamship *Comet*.

It was met by senior officials including the Mayor, Mr Doughty of Upton, and Mr G.W.Ledgard, who provided the carriages in which the King proceeded to Lulworth Castle to stay with the Weld family. On seeing the castle he is reputed to have exclaimed: "Voilá la Bastille" – hardly a compliment to his hosts. After two months he was removed to Scotland, but meanwhile the majority of his small army of camp followers were accommodated in Poole. The inhabitants turned out in large numbers to have a look at the exiled despot and no missiles were thrown. It was a free entertainment and a unique one, for the French Charles brought with him a fair sample of the cream of his country's nobility. They included one princess, three countesses, three duchesses, three dukes, two barons, five counts, five valets, the King's doctor,and several other nobles besides cooks, footmen and maids-in-waiting, also two teachers and two "keepers of the plate".

This was a time when Dorset farm labourers, living at subsistence level, frequently set fire to cottages, barns and farmhouses. In Poole too, life in the political sphere was decidedly stormy. In the early 1830s the Corporation consisted of a Mayor, four Aldermen and twenty-eight Burgesses who elected two members of Parliament. In 1830 Poole was represented by William Ponsonby and Benjamin Lester, who were both in favour of electoral reform, the most controversial issue just then, Benjamin L. Lester had played a prominent part in the great Poole-Newfoundland fishery.

William Ponsonby was the brother of Caroline who married the favourite son of Lord Melbourne. Thus she became the famous and notorious Caroline Lamb who described Byron as "mad, bad and dangerous to know". As far as Caroline was concerned, the description turned out to be too near the truth to be for her good.

William Ponsonby inherited Canford Manor and built the stone mansion that stands there today as Canford School. Unlike his predecessors, the

Webbes, he was well disposed towards Poole and an agreement was reached on boundaries which gave the town room to expand. Nor was this his only act of generosity towards Poole. In 1830 he was responsible for the building of the first public library, a project first proposed at a meeting three years earlier, when it was suggested that a library would produce results "for which posterity will venerate our memory". The same year, 1827, saw the foundation of the Bethel Company, a sort of nineteenth century Mission to Seamen. Its object was to provide twelve members who would visit ships and seamen belonging to the port of Poole. "Lending ship libraries" were to be established for their benefit. "The new public library, built at the bottom of the High Street" was one of the changes that Philip Gosse noted when he returned from Newfoundland in 1830. The Reform Bill of 1832 provided for only a modest extension of the right to vote. A census taken in 1821 showed the population of Poole to be 6,390. Of these only 126 people were entitled to vote. After the Reform Bill, the electorate, based on property, totalled 540. Yet those early elections aroused passions which sometimes burst into violence. Meetings were disrupted and officals accused of vote-rigging and bribery. In spite of all this, only a small percentage of those entitled to vote bothered to do so.

The constituency boundaries now included Hamworthy, Longfleet and Parkstone, an enlargement which was by no means universally welcomed. The Dorset County Chronicle was of the opinion that the addition of the new suburbs would cause Poole to "lose its independence" and continued: "Poole is a place of no mean importance. In point of respectability few towns surpass it ... it contains about 8,000 inhabitants. Why are they not considered of sufficient intelligence to choose their own representatives without assistance?"

The newspaper also suggested that the redrawn boundaries were "a cloak for corruption and nomination" – but in spite of these misgivings the new constituency boundaries were duly confirmed by law.

As may be seen from the map Hamworthy is only separated from Poole by a narrow neck of water where Poole Quay is situated – a matter of less than three hundred feet. Until the building of the bridge, the only connection was by a small boat, so Poole and Hamworthy were effectively separated.

Strange as it seems to us today, the majority of the people were opposed to the linking up of the two places. One objection was that the piers of a bridge would affect the tidal flow, possibly decreasing the depth outside the quays. In this respect the fears may have been groundless, but the objectors were not altogether wrong, since one result of building the bridge was a sharp drop in the value of property on the Poole side.

Eventually Poole Council decided in favour of the bridge and Parliament passed the necessary Bill in 1834. The MP for Poole, William Ponsonby, was not only the chief promoter of the bridge project, he even paid for it out of his own pocket to the tune of £9,611.13s. It lasted until 1885. The third bridge was opened by Alderman Herbert Carter in 1927. When the first bridge was opened a local commentator expressed the opinion that the greatest industrial development in the Poole area would now take place at Hamworthy. History has proved him wrong, in spite of the tremendous importance of the cross-channel terminal at Hamworthy, that essential link in the Poole-Cherbourg trade.

In this year, 1834, the most common trade in Poole was that of baker and flour dealer, if we can rely on a contemporary commercial directory. There were eighteen of them, while grocers numbered twelve, boot and shoe repairers fifteen and hairdressers five. Of taverns and public houses there were thirty-five, the same number as ten years earlier, when they included the Air Balloon and the Bakers Arms, the latter well-known to smugglers.

The stage coach was still the mainstay of transport. At six o'clock every morning *The Age* left the Old Antelope Hotel for London and three times a week at half past six the *Wellington* left the same hotel for Bath and Bristol. A coach running to Weymouth and Southampton called twice a week at the London Hotel. There was also a busy coastal trade carried largely by vessels owned in Poole. All this was to change with dramatic suddenness.

In 1845 the Bristol, Bath and Poole Railway Company issued its prospectus. It offered 50,000 shares at £10 each and stated that the Company, with a capital of one million pounds, would be devoted "to the improvement of the harbour of Poole which from its very favourable position can at a trifling outlay be rendered the most sheltered, safest and most commodious port in the Southern Kingdom".

In November of the next year the following notice was published in the press:

> *Bristol and Poole Harbour Railway*
> *Notice is hereby given that the ACTING*
> *COMMITTEE of the Company will proceed*
> *on the 13th day of December next to*
> *allot the several SHARES .*
> *Castleman and Kingdon*
> *Secretaries.*

These were two among numerous small companies in a hurry to jump on the new railway bandwagon. The line duly reached Poole in May 1846, winding its way from Southampton through Redbridge, Lyndhurst, Brockenhurst, Ringwood, Wimborne and Wareham, so earning for itself the nickname "Castleman's Corkscrew". Poole station was on the Hamworthy side of the Quay. The engine which drew the first train was called *Reindeer* and the reporter from the Poole and Dorchester Herald was enthusiastic about the first run. "The riding was particularly easy on the Rockley Bridge," he wrote, "which is nearly a quarter of a mile long." Probably he felt some anxiety as to whether the new contraption would get safely across. He need not have worried. Within weeks the stage coach services had gone out of business; and so, a little later, had Poole's coastal shipping. Until the railways came, some twenty vessels entered Poole every week and a similar number sailed out. But though the long-distance coaches such as *Forrester* and *Emerald* would no longer run to London and Southampton, some of them would find a place in the local services now spreading through Dorset and Hampshire.

People were quite aware of the fact that they were living in the middle of an industrial revolution and they worked with enormous energy to further the process. A writer in the Poole and Dorsetshire Herald of 1846 reflects on the difference between the revolution sought by Napoleon thirty years earlier and the scientific one promoted by the English and Scots. In 1788, this writer says, a year before the French Revolution, the first experimental steamboat was being tried out on a remote Scottish loch. This was to have far greater effect on men's lives, he reflects, than the political upheavals in France.

The same issue of the Herald says that "an experiment is to be made to establish telegraphic communication between England and France by means of a wire laid on the sea bed".

Another, if lesser, sign of the times appears as an advertisement on the front page:

> *Every person should use PIKE'S*
> *newly invented metallic pens. 6d.*
> *per dozen. Warranted not to patch or*
> *sprinkle. On sale at Sydenham's, Poole.*

Also on the front page Mr Horatio Hamilton, dentist, offers his services "at his residence in the High Street", and during these early decades of the century there were usually about five surgeons practising in Poole. By 1871 their number had decreased to three. The crude surgery that had been practised for hundreds of years was fading out as modern medicine advanced. The barber-surgeons who advertised their services would only tackle quite simple and superficial operations, such as the removal of carbuncles and of course bleeding, which was done either with leeches or by opening a vein. There were a few distinguished pioneers in surgery, but on the whole the practice of medicine was primitive in our modern view and the idea of hygiene was in its infancy. At Guy's Hospital in 1735 a Mr John Hilberdine was paid £20 "on account of his services in killing buggs". He earned as much as the surgeons and doctors and conditions were not much different a hundred years later.

In front of one of the wards of St Bartholomew's Hospital in the eighteenth century was an open cesspool into which all kinds of waste matter was dumped. The Thames reached its peak as a sewer as the nineteenth century went on and the population of London grew. It was four hundred years since the keepers of Henry VIII's tame polar bear had been able to let it out on a long chain to catch fish, including salmon, in the Thames.

Poole was spared the worst evils of the Industrial Revolution, but not without paying a certain price; for local industry could not compete with more advanced factory production. This was a contributory factor in the decline of Poole's trade with Newfoundland. However, one unqualified benefit of advancing technology was the advent of gas. The Poole Gas and Coke Company was formed in 1833 with a capital of £4,000 and the following year the streets of Poole were lit by gas. A leaflet was printed on "The Advantages of the Gas Meter". The alternative was that the customer should agree to put his lights out at a certain time every night, and that the flame should not be above a certain height.

On the advertisement pages the trade of gas fitter begins to appear regularly. Messrs Farmer and Co. offered their services as "bell-hangers, furnishers and gas-fitters". If gas could be a sideline of furnishers, tea was still sufficiently a novelty to be treated by grocers as a separate commodity. Some shopkeepers described themselves simply as 'grocers', while others were 'grocers and tea dealers'.

Throughout the century, about twenty grocers are listed and second to them in numbers come boot and shoe repairers, while in mid-century it seems that almost anybody could set up as a "beer retailer", for in 1859 seventeen of them are listed. In the same period there were no fewer than thirty agents representing the same number of Insurance and Assurance companies. The presence and the proliferation of small retailers reflects the growing population of the town. In 1859 there were over 300 shopkeepers and merchants. Poole's special trades of sail-making, rope-making and ship and boat building carried steadily on and of course there were potteries springing up to make use of the local clay.

Kelly's Directory for this year mentions that Poole "possesses a most pleasing suburb in the direction of Parkstone, commanding extensive prospects of the harbour of Poole, The Isle of Purbeck and the west end of the Isle of Wight ... Several new public buildings have been erected: the church of St James in 1820, the chapel of Ham, built in 1826 on the site of a chapel destroyed in the Civil War; the church at Parkstone erected in 1833 and the church at Longfleet in the same year. The living at St James, a perpetual curacy, valued in 1835 at £307 is in the gift of what is known as Simeon's Trustees. The Rev. Peter William Jolliffe is the present incumbent and is between 90 and 100 years of age.

"This parish also contains a district church called St Paul's; an independent chapel seating about 1,400 persons; a large Baptist and also a Weslyan chapel; also a Unitarian Meeting, Primitive Methodist, Quakers and Catholic chapel."

This flourishing of nonconformist religious movements was all in the tradition of Poole radicalism. It was because the Established Church had become remote, over-respectable, out of touch with the mass of the people and unable to cope with a swiftly changing society in which Wesleyanism, Evangelicalism and other reformist Christian movements had sprung up to bring Christianity into the everyday lives of ordinary people. Its message overlapped with that of political radicalism and reform, and its influence may be traced in such twentieth-century leaders as George Lansbury and Aneurin Bevan.

"Steam communication is now established between this town and Cherbourg," proclaims a writer in 1867. "The passage occupies about six hours." This time compares very well with our modern Truckline diesel-engined ships which make the sixty-seven miles crossing in four-and-a-half hours. Partly owing to poor management, the 1867 shipping company did not last long. It has always been difficult for Poole to compete for passengers with Southampton to the east so near to London, and Weymouth for the West Country.

On the lighter side of going afloat there was the annual regatta. Reports of the 1840 and 1841 events show that the arrangements differed mainly in scale. Yachts were divided into classes and there was a race for fishing boats and one for "clay and market boats". "The shore opposite Brownsea was lined with carriages and horsemen." As the future Poole Park was a swamp, these spectators must have been watching from the eastern end of the quay and Baiter peninsula.

The spread of the railways in late Victorian times transformed the life of those days as dramatically as cars and motorways have changed ours. Christmas cards which depict stage coaches stuck in the snow and laughing passengers waving bottles out of the windows are a romantic delusion. As soon as jolly John Bull and his wife were offered a railway coach instead they jumped into it, hard though the seats were.

By 1871 the South Western Railway was offering services "to Bournemouth daily, to and from the London Hotel, High Street. Trains from Poole eleven times each way; Samuel Pettet, Station Master". An omnibus collected passengers from the London Hotel, took them to the station and also brought arrivals from the station to the hotel. Clearly Bournemouth was growing in size and importance. Twenty-five years earlier there were only two hotels, although the Poole and Dorset Herald recommended its "sea-bathing and sea air in all their excellence". But tourism in 1846 was on so small a scale that the same newspaper gives the names of twenty married couples under "Recent arrivals".

The year 1885 was an important one for Poole in regard to the harbour and its once splendid oyster fishery. In this year the Poole Harbour Act appointed the Harbour Commissioners, a body to be composed of the Lord Mayor and six councillors plus one representative each for Wareham, the landowners, the tradesmen, the fishermen and the railways. Henceforth the Corporation was once more able to control the dredging of oysters and so the over-exploited shellfish began to recover their numbers. Two years later two hundred acres on the Wareham Channel were leased to a local company for the cultivation of oysters.

Poole Park was opened in 1890 by the Prince of Wales, the future Edward VII. It was a gift from Lord Wimborne, the Lord of the Manor of

Canford at that time. The Corporation also came to an agreement with Lord Wimborne that an area of land at Lilliput should be converted by him into a golf course, while Poole was to have the use of land formerly the site of a waterworks.

The Poole Park lakes are situated in the area where the Town Gates and wall were built. In past centuries these shallow inlets reached far inland so as to come within fifty yards or so of Holes Bay on the eastern side, so creating the peninsula on which the town of Poole was situated. A writer in the *Town Guide* for 1910 describes this area as it was before the Park was made: "Forty years ago, Poole Park consisted of a small farm on the higher ground and a few marshy meadows over which a precarious footpath wound its devious way ... the waterlogged part has been drained and the water collected into pretty little lakes with willowy islands where there are stately swans and quaint Egyptian geese and other waterfowl ... the marsh where the present writer in his youth sought for water plants while the snipe hummed around and the haunting cry of the lapwing pursued the course of the intruder, is now a splendid cricket ground, so good that the great county cricket matches are played there."

This was one more stage in the reclamation of parts of the eastern fringe of the harbour. But Poole was to continue its historic expansion in a far more dramatic way: in 1905 the Town Council amalgamated with Branksome Urban District Council. Thus the Borough of Poole pushed out its boundaries in a south-easterly direction to claim what is now a most select and sought-after area. It stretches right down to the beach at Branksome Chine, but two miles from Bournemouth pier. It was open to Bournemouth to acquire the Branksome area but at that time those barren miles of scrub and sandy soil did not seem very desirable. It was only after much heated debate that Poole took the far-sighted step.

Branksome Chine itself was bought only in 1929 and again there was much argument before the decision was taken. The Chine had become a sort of shanty town for holidaymakers, as Sandbanks did in the early 'twenties. Now this was replaced by pleasure gardens which were opened in 1930 by Margaret Bondfield, the first woman to be a member of the Cabinet. Then a Solarium was built at the foot of the Chine and opened in 1932, but it failed to attract the public and was turned into a cafe.

The number of town councillors now increased from twenty-four to thirty-six and they decided that the old Guildhall was no longer big enough. They also voted a pony and trap for the borough engineer. These developments prompted Councillor Browne to declare that "between their desire to propitiate Branksome and endeavour to satisfy the appetites of local cormorants, the committee now wish to launch the municipal ship upon a sea of reckless extravagance".

In these Edwardian days the great political conflict was between Conservatives and Liberals. Mention has been made of the intensity of party battles at the time of the Reform Bill of 1832 and the physical violence which sometimes occurred. In 1906 Tories tried to overrun the platform occupied by prominent Liberals and were hurled back. To find such political passions today one has to look to parties of the extreme left and right, such as the Socialist Workers' Party and the National Front.

The most common offence in those days was to be "drunk and disorderly"; today it would be illegal parking. Drunkenness called into being the Temperance Societies, several of which met frequently in Poole. In 1913 the Grand Chief Templar of the Order of Rechabites visited Poole to address the united forces of teetotalism. In 1908 Councillor G Watkin proposed a motion to censure the Mayor for making uncomplimentary remarks about the liquor trade. Again the champions of temperance turned up in force and the motion was heavily defeated. In 1912 Poole Council passed a resolution that no drinks of any kind, alcoholic or otherwise, should be served in the Park on Sundays. Blessed are they who thirst after righteousness ... but in 1911 large quantities of beer were consumed at the festivities to celebrate the coronation of George V, a lapse from sobriety which horrified many people.

Temperance was closely allied to the dissenting factions of the Christian Church, now focussed in the Unitarian Church in Hill Street, formerly the Great Meeting House built in 1704 and rebuilt about 1860. The Unitarians were the heirs of the original Dissenters who broke away from St James Church to follow the Revd Samuel Hardy into the 'wilderness'. So strong were religious feelings even in this pre-1913 decade that several councillors, some of them magistrates, refused to pay their rates as a protest against Church of England teaching in schools.

Battles raged not only over teetotalism and forms of worship but over many developments which we have learned to take for granted: sanitation, the water supply, hospitals, education. The Parkstone School for Boys and Girls was founded in 1905 by Mr W.E.Brennand; but Mr Brennand opposed the founding of a Secondary Municipal School which Poole Council had advocated.

The Adult Education movement spread from Bournemouth to Poole in 1905 and hundreds attended meetings at Amity Hall and Emerson Hall. Lively discussions based on biblical texts took place and with sports and excursions the classes developed into a sort of club.

Like the demand for better education, the need for better medical services was also making itself felt, and in 1907 Cornelia, Lady Wimborne opened the new Cornelia Hospital which replaced the inadequate accommodation of the old Sir Peter Thompson mansion in Market Street. Another step forward was the appointment of a medical officer to tend to schoolchildren.

In 1910 the water supply was reorganised with the installation of a new pumping station at Corfe Mullen. This was the successful outcome of a campaign during which there had been exhibited at meetings glass jars of tapwater in which there thrived various forms of pond life.

The fire-fighting service was another controversial issue. There was no full-time service, and horses were hired from bakers and brewers. The new chemical extinguishers aroused deep suspicion and there was even more heated argument over the purchase of a motorised fire engine in 1913. The petrol engine had barely started its career, and the same could be said of the aeroplane. In 1910 Mr Rolls, the financial backer of Mr Royce, died in an air crash when he was taking part in an aerial display off Bournemouth. One year earlier, M.Bleriot had made the first flight across the Channel.

Nevertheless, as early as 1911 Poole's Mayor Herbert Carter owned a 'baby' Peugeot. To supplement the Peugeot he bought a donkey complete with a small wagon and harness for £8.10s. In his memoirs Herbert Carter describes how they organised a race between the donkey and the motor car from Poole to Worth Matravers, a village a few miles west of Swanage. The donkey started a day earlier and spent the night at Corfe. "The Peugeot overhauled the donkey before Kingston was reached, but engine trouble delayed the car ... and Jeremiah ambled past the finishing post, winner by a few lengths." At Worth, the donkey's duty was to carry the children along the steep, winding trail to and from Chapman's Pool. "He would frequently sigh deeply and lie down in the middle of the road."

The long-suffering, often irritable but likeable donkey used to be very much a part of the daily scene, helping with jobs which did not require the strength of a horse. When in 1912 my grandmother bought a cottage at Sandbanks, there was at the bottom of the garden a flimsy building called "the donkey shed" and though we never kept a donkey the previous householders may well have done so. There was a donkey on Green Island right into the 1930s.

Descriptions of life in late Victorian and Edwardian times tend to give an impression of security, peace and plenty. 'Plenty' however was not for everyone, and at the end of Victoria's reign peace was interrupted by the South African War. In that heyday of British power it was possible for a patriotic citizen to write to the Poole and Dorset Herald:

> *Undaunted yet and undismayed*
> *The lion stands at bay*
> *And the lion's cubs are gathered round*
> *All ready for the fray;*
> *No time is this for craven fears*
> *No time is this for woman's tears*
> *'Tis England calls us on with cheers*
> *To arms! To arms! To arms!*

In the same year, 1900, a patriotic concert was held at the Amity Hall, a building which later became a cinema. The programme included "Songs by Mrs Gwatkin, Mrs Young and Mrs Ireland Blackburne. Violin solos by Signor Bertoncini and Mrs Goodger". Wars were still remote and far away, and won by men with rifles and bayonets; and Poole Breweries were advertising bitter ale at a shilling, pale ale at 1/6d and old at two shillings per gallon.

The Golden Age, if such it was, had only a few years to run before the 1914 war blew it sky high, together with so many other illusions. In what way can the part played by a minor seaport be distinguished from the efforts of every other part of the country? There was the not negligible shipbuilding industry to be guarded, mainly against the possibility of an instrusive submarine, and so a guard ship was stationed in the main channel, just south of Brownsea Island. From this vessel there drifted across the water to Sandbanks the screechy tone of a primitive gramophone playing "Who were you with last night?" and "Hallo, who's your lady friend?"

Poole became a naval port with many trawlers converted into minesweepers. There were rumours that the periscope of a U-boat had been seen in Poole Bay. Poole's own shipbuilding industry contributed a steel naval lighter for carrying ammunition and built by Bolsons, while in August 1918 the same firm built the first ship in Britain to be constructed of reinforced concrete. The Lady Mayoress performed the launching ceremony and the Daily Mirror called the craft "the first of a concrete fleet that will still further dash the sinking hopes of the Huns". Such was the enthusiasm aroused by one concrete barge.

It was followed by a seagoing tug built of the same material, but results were not encouraging and the trail that had promised to lead to a fleet of concrete ships turned out to be a dead end.

British shipping losses reached their peak in 1918, and food shortages were at their worst. The Poole fishing fleet still brought its catch home, but nearly all of it was sent to London and the Poole fishmongers displayed notices saying "No Fish". This was naturally resented by the local population who began an agitation to keep locally caught fish in Poole.

It was not only the fishmongers who displayed notices saying they had nothing to offer. The depressing announcements could be seen all down the High Street – "No Cheese", "No Tea", "No Jam", "No Margarine". Butchers opened on only one or two days a week, and the lines of women standing outside food shops grew longer.

One of the wartime functions of the Port of Poole was to receive and store cargoes of ammunition. Some of these cargoes were damaged by sea water and had to be destroyed. Also arriving, but by rail, were casualties from the Western Front requiring hospital treatment.

Peace came in 1918, and with it the influenza epidemic which killed more millions than did the war. The editor of the Poole and Dorset Herald and his wife were among its victims, dying within a week of one another. So heavy were the fatalities that hundreds of victims had to be buried without coffins.

In the same year the former Prime Minister of Newfoundland, Lord Morris, visited Poole and initiated a movement to revive the great fishery business between Poole and Newfoundland. One might as well have tried to bring back the sailing ships too! There was simply no longer any commercial incentive to base the fisheries at Poole.

The festivities celebrating peace in 1919 included refreshments and games for six hundred children in the Park, a procession of ex-servicemen through the town and a bonfire on Constitution Hill. But all was not fun and games. Teachers demonstrated for higher pay and the threat of rioting by the unemployed was taken so seriously that a party of marines was landed at Poole to forestall any attempt to damage property. Then as now there was a housing problem, and this question was the subject of a heated debate in the Council in December 1919.

Another armed detachment landed at Poole in 1921, brought by a destroyer, to guard the ammunition factory at Holton Heath. These were times of great unrest. In July 1921 crowds of unemployed thronged the streets. Their number in the Poole district was estimated at two thousand. One of their demands was that children should be given meals at school. This demand was in fact granted, thanks to a charitable organisation called the Guild of Hope. The Welfare State was still twenty-five years away; and Women's Lib was an even more distant prospect.

In 1925 the Corporation dismissed a schoolteacher, Mrs Short, on the grounds that a wife's place is in the home. The case was tried in London and Mrs Short lost. The large number of men out of work counted against her. But she later founded a successful school of her own.

Since late Victorian times the possibility of creating a school of art in Poole had been discussed from time to time. In 1925 it actually came into existence, and was housed in three huts, with Mr Percy Wise as its director.

Progress in the material sphere was more ambitious. In 1923 the Bournemouth-Swanage Motor Road and Traction Company was incorporated. This was the company which established the chain ferry across the harbour mouth and built the road from Shell Bay to Studland. Opposition came mainly from the fishermen, who feared collisions between their boats and the ferry. Their fears were not groundless, but the number of collisions has been small, and fishermen are too experienced to tangle with the steel monster, captive on its chains. The ferry went into service in 1926.

In this year when the "floating bridge" was inaugurated, Poole Bridge, the link with Hamworthy, was demolished. The new bridge was opened on 9 March 1927. In the same year the Corporation bought Scaplen's Court, the most historic building in Poole, and now a museum.

In 1927 the War Memorial in Poole Park was unveiled. There had been much heated argument in the Council as to what form the memorial should take.

In 1929 Lord Baden Powell was given the freedom of the Borough. He was entertained to lunch at the Guildhall with his wife, whose home town was Parkstone.

The Lord Mayor of London, Sir Phene Neal, laid the foundation stone of the new municipal buildings, arriving with attendants and regalia in two state coaches. Opened in 1931, these buildings are generally considered to be a fine example of the better architecture of that period. On the outer walls a series of carved stone panels illustrates Poole's history. Local artists thus recorded the potters of the Stone Age, the Roman invasion by sea, Saxon galleys and the seamen of later years.

In the same year Hamworthy Park was opened, with its paddling pool, boating lake and lovely views of the harbour. Its beach, the north side of the Wareham Channel, had already gone through the curious transformation of mud to sand which is still in progress throughout the harbour.

Evidently there was considerable progress between the wars on the national as well as on the local scale. The Poole fishing fleet might be said to symbolise this transitional period, as it consisted of solid, broad, thirty-five feet cutter-rigged boats with rugged engines doing a fifty-fifty job with good old-fashioned canvas sails smelling of creosote.

Municipal Buildings, Parkstone, drawn by Sheila Sturdy in 1949. These offices were built in 1932, between Commercial Road (left) and Sandbanks Road (with the street cleaner). The northern gates into Poole Park are also sketched (near right).

WAR and PEACE

A MERE twenty years intervened between the Armistice celebrations of 1919 and Mr Neville Chamberlain's melancholy wireless announcement on the first September Sunday of 1939 that "we are at war with Germany".

As in past centuries, England was never invaded by the enemy, but for Poole there was an invasion of children from London, Southampton and other strategically-placed cities. Already short of schools and houses, Poole was now called upon to accommodate thousands of extra bodies. Teachers had to cope with double shifts in the classrooms and on the playing fields. It seemed an almost impossible task, yet somehow they accomplished it.

Apart from that very little happened, and everyone began to wonder whether anything much ever would happen. The answer came in the spring of 1940 when the Germans drove the British Expeditionary Force to the beaches of Dunkirk, together with thousands of French troops. Suddenly Poole Harbour was crowded with Dutch ships and boats, taking refuge from their enemy-occupied ports. A Dutch merchant vessel was sunk by a magnetic mine in the Swash Channel, and until quite recently its remains could still be seen at low spring tides on the western edge of Hook Sands.

These Dutch vessels were to play their part in the next act of the drama, the big lift-off of troops from the beaches of Dunkirk. Fishermen, ferrymen and all owners of small craft were ordered to prepare themselves for a special task, the nature of which they could only guess at. Towards the end of May 1940 there assembled in Studland Bay a fleet of small boats which included fishing trawlers, ferry boats including some owned by the Harvey and Davis families, and three of the 'Skylarks', which were very sturdy open motor boats and ran a service for tourists between Poole and Bournemouth. There were also a type of craft from Holland called schuits, These were small boats normally used for the transport of sand, peat and other cargoes along the inland waterways.

The Poole lifeboat was among this fleet which was escorted round the coast to Dover, a journey of some two hundred miles. It took twenty-eight hours, the convoy being under the command of Captain H.Quick. But when the Poole men reached Dover their boats were taken over and manned by the Royal Navy.

Soon there were French soldiers billeted in Poole and Bournemouth, and on Brownsea Island a group of Dutch refugees was accommodated in marquees. A filtration plant was set up and water brought from the lake some seven hundred yards away. These fugitives from the Nazi fury told horrifying tales of their flight, during which they had been strafed by machine-gun fire. Their number included a burgomaster, a musician, a banker and a doctor who said he had once attended Queen Wilhelmina. Later they were moved away to different parts of the country.

The war had started in earnest. A strict blackout was already in force and the Council decided to avoid the additional labour and expense of a modified form of blackout, which was the alternative. The unfortunate aspect of this was that people frequently stepped off the quay and found themselves swimming for their lives. At least two unfortunate citizens were drowned in this way. Then in 1942 the danger was circumvented by the erection of fencing.

Poole and Bournemouth now came within what was called a restricted or defence area. It applied to a twenty-mile deep belt of coast where invasion could be expected, and checkpoints were set up on all roads leading to this coastal area. At Sandbanks everyone was liable to be given twenty-four hours' notice to move out altogether.

The impact of these developments was felt most severely by the hotel business, which was brought almost to a halt. A tribunal was appointed by the government to decide which hotel managements could be exempted from paying rates.

During these wartime years Poole and Bournemouth were always referred to in the press as "a south coast town" when such matters as air raids and military defences were being reported. For example, in July 1940 "Mr Winston Churchill visited south coast defences ... he took tea in one of the most charming hotels on the south coast, looking down across the heath to beautiful sand with the white cliffs of England also noticeable. This great man – the implacable foe of the upstart clique of tyrants in Berlin – made a thorough inspection of the work". Mr Churchill was casting a critical eye on the plans for repelling any invaders who might attempt to land on Studland's golden beaches and swarm across the heath.

It was said in those days that the Government was spending five million pounds a day on the war. It may therefore seem strange that the public should be asked to dig into its pocket and contribute still more. Yet that is what happened. There was the Spitfire Fund in 1940 and later Warship Week to raise money to pay for torpedo boats. In October 1940 it was announced that Poole had succeeded in paying for one Spitfire with the sum of £5,000. The town also passed its target in Warship Week by raising over half-a-million pounds. Two years later the British citizen was asked to raise money for medical aid to Russia and all kinds of aid to China against the Japanese. Poole contributed £2,200.

"Poole's 1940 story will not set the history books ablaze," commented a writer in the Poole and Dorset Herald in that year. The enemy however did his best to set Poole ablaze. On 15-16 April hundreds of fire bombs were dropped on the town. They did little damage, thanks to the numbers and efficiency of fire-watchers – seventeen thousand of them in the Poole/Bournemouth area. At this stage of the war fire-watching was voluntary, but in August 1942 it became compulsory for women to play their part in this branch of defence.

Later in the year squadrons of German bombers passed over Poole almost nightly and the peace of the night was shattered by anti-aircraft fire and air raid sirens. The bombers passed on their way to targets in the Midlands and North. However bombs were occasionally dropped in the Poole area, and parachute mines caused some damage and casualties.

In the centre of the south coast, the Poole/Bournemouth area was as vulnerable to invasion as any stretch of coast in Britain, and there were no half measures about the anti-invasion defences. Lightning raids might be made at any moment from the Cherbourg peninsula, a mere seventy miles across the water.

The naval officer in charge at Poole was Commander C.B.Hastings, a veteran of the 1914 war. His HQ was the motor cruiser *Florinda*, once the first club-house of the Royal Motor Yacht Club. He had a boom placed across the mouth of the harbour, a task carried out by Lieutenant Commander Vandy, aided by Captain Carey from Portland. Gathering materials wherever they could find them, these enterprising officers not only constructed a boom across the harbour mouth but equipped it with explosive charges which could be discharged by remote control. It was Commander Vandy's son Harry who devised this scheme. The timber came from trees felled on Brownsea, which naturally distressed the nature-loving owner, Mrs Florence Bonham Christie. Harry says of those days that in spite of all this defence activity nobody took the threat of invasion very seriously.

In addition to the explosive boom, a patrol vessel checked every ship in the harbour approaches and was in radio contact with the gun batteries based on shore. Up in the harbour shallows an old ship lay ready to be towed into the middle of the main channel. She was laden with explosives and could be blown up and sunk to block the channel. Within the harbour ordinary ferryboats went on patrol armed with machine-guns.

At this time the Local Defence Volunteers became the Home Guard. They were under the command of a retired Army officer, Sir Mervyn Wheatley, and their orders were to retreat fighting, even ultimately to Scotland.

Rolls of barbed wire ran the length of the local beaches, on which no member of the public was allowed to set foot. Later the wire was replaced by tubular scaffolding. Anti-tank barriers were built at strategic points and anti-aircraft guns were positioned in Poole Park and on Baiter peninsula and Constitution Hill. Six old cars were filled with explosive and placed beneath Fleets Bridge. As a defence against aerial invasion posts or steel piping were driven into the ground wherever open spaces might offer a landing site, a system extended even to the shallows of the harbour. If the invaders did arrive, important plants such as Hamworthy Engineering had their plans ready to destroy vital installations.

There were not only boats on the harbour, there were flying boats. Soon after the outbreak of war, Imperial Airways left Hythe and established its headquarters at Poole. Landing and takeoff were made on the long, exposed stretch of the Wareham Channel off Hamworthy, where the prevailing westerly winds were a helpful feature. Poole Harbour Yacht Club was taken over as the Marine Terminal from which customs and medical staff operated. Incoming passengers were received in a part of the Poole Potteries premises on the Quay.

The flights of the flying boats from Poole were not numerous, but they were important in keeping open lines of communication between allies all across the world at a time when Britain was a rather lonely island in a hostile sea. And some of those flights were vital links in a chain of success. One of them was made by Captain Donald Bennett, later to found the Pathfinders and become an Air Vice-Marshal. His hazardous task was to fly General Sikorsi to France, whence the Polish leader had to make his way to Poland. The flight took place on 20 June 1940. Captain Bennett brought his flying boat down on the lake at Biscarosse, about thirty miles south of Bordeaux. The French were still at the small seaplane base there, but had sunk their aircraft in the lake. An air raid shortly after Captain Bennett's arrival caused him some anxiety as to the safety of his aircraft, which he had taxied in amongst the trees on the lake shores.

The following day General Sikorski and his chiefs of staff arrived back and embarked, and on 21 June the flying boat took off, arriving back at Poole at nine o'clock in the morning. It seems amazing that Captain Bennett's aircraft was not fired on by the Germans, who were present in considerable numbers around the lake at Biscarosse, complete with tanks and armoured vehicles. Ironically it was a British cruiser which fired at the flying boat just outside Bordeaux.

Another historic flight from Poole took the French General Larminat to the Congo. There he was able to organise the seizure of Brazzaville which had been under the control of the German puppet government in France. This success made it possible for British air services to fly south and across Africa to the Middle East and Australia.

It was a flying boat that snatched King Peter of Yugoslavia from the wartime turmoil in his country and took him to Cairo. Thence another plane brought him to Poole.

The continual activity of flying boats based at Poole led to the development of a company which is still active in the area, Flight Refuelling Ltd., a name descriptive of its original purpose.

In 1941 Adolf Hitler was in his eighth year of unbroken success and commanded an empire that stretched from the Pyrenees to the Arctic Circle. America was not yet in the war; Britain stood in enfeebled and apparently hopeless isolation. Then the German dictator made his fatal mistake and marched his legions into the Russian morass.

At this stage of the war the Commando units were founded and a detachment of them trained at Poole under Major Gustavus March-Phillips, DSO, who was later killed in Normandy and was succeeded by Major Appleyard. Their HQ was in the Antelope Hotel in Poole High Street and their training was done on a converted Brixham trawler called *Maid Honor*. In August 1941 they set off in this sailing boat for West Africa to spy on the movements of German U-boats. They also boarded and captured the Italian liner *Duchessa d'Aorta*. Returning to Poole they underwent further training and took part in raids on the Normandy coast and on the island of Sark.

The spring of 1941 was the worst period for air raids experienced by Poole. For the ordinary civilian there were many sleepless nights and a certain amount of damage was done both by high-explosive and incendiary bombs. The Branksome gasworks was hit and so was Beales, the Bournemouth department store. Raids became less frequent, however, when the main German effort was switched to the Russian front. It remained for the average citizen to soldier on and make the best of the food rations, the ban on all private motoring and on meals costing more than five shillings. It was forbidden to use water on gardens and the public were advised never to fill a bath beyond a depth of six inches, in the interests of saving fuel. Certain areas of public parks were turned over to growing vegetables, and even parts of cemeteries were used for the same purpose. It was still a question of holding on, though the higher authorities realised there was now little possibility of an invasion.

The Home Guard was increasing in numbers and had almost reached 3,000 in 1942. Brownsea Island had been turned into a decoy for enemy bombers by the installation of lights and explosives on its north-west cliffs. The lights simulated those of Poole while the electrically detonated explosives gave the pilots the illusion that their leaders had bombed the target area. In May of that year Poole would have suffered appalling damage had it not been for the Brownsea decoy which on one occasion absorbed by far the greater part of a massive attack.

In 1943 Poole was playing its role as a seaport to the limit of its capacity. Small ships came from hundreds of miles away for repair. Bolsons built a minesweeper, as did the Dorset Yacht Company: and they were also building landing craft. In Poole Bay experiments were carried out with pipelines carrying petrol in preparation for those which would take fuel across the Channel after the invasion of Normandy. Pipelines later pumped fuel from several British ports across the Channel and far into continental Europe. These floating pipelines were rolled on and off cone-ended drums known as 'conundrums'.

The Naval establishment in and around Poole was known as *HMS Turtle*. It was a land-based 'turtle' and comprised Green and Furzey Islands, and by 1943 the number of men and women attached to it had reached some 4,000. The harbour, vacated in 1940, was now crowded again but with ships of war instead of pleasure yachts. In fact it became too crowded for the flying boats, and four months prior to the invasion they moved to Wales. The fleet of small vessels in the harbour included some whose function would be to ferry supplies across the Channel. There were gunboats, torpedo boats and different types of landing craft numbering in excess of three hundred. To these were soon added sixty American coastguard cutters eighty-three feet in length.

To cater for the American forces the old Guildhall had already been converted into an American Red Cross Club. The Sheriff of Poole had presided over the opening ceremony at which the US representative was Mr Clarence C. Cline. "We are grateful for your lightning response to our appeal," said Mr Cline. "We gladly accept ye olde ancient monument, the Guildhall of Poole, to be run as an American Red Cross Club."

When on 6 June 1944 the invasion fleet moved out, the people of the Dorset coastal regions walked to the cliffs to look seawards at this historic event, as they had done at the time of the Spanish Armada. In 1944 the extraordinary fleet included two old battleships which would be sunk to form an artificial breakwater. From Poole a ferry service continued to operate across the Channel, carrying fuel and supplies.

In September 1944 the Poole Home Guard went on parade for the last time and their compulsory training was brought to an end. In the same month the Mayor of Poole welcomed the first batch of prisoners of war to return from the Far East by air and these were followed by further arrivals every day.

About twenty-four flying boats were now operating from Poole, and only moved to Southampton in 1947. The enterprising Mrs Louie Dingwall (Miss Foott) of Sandbanks ran a taxi service for the crews to and from London. Every night the mail had to be collected and brought back to Poole in time to catch the 05.00 plane back to America. Mrs Dingwall often drove her 40 hp Packard herself.

From 1 March 1945 sailing was permitted on the east side of the harbour. The war in Europe ended on 8 May 1945, though peace in the Pacific was not declared until 14 August. In May there were thanksgiving services and celebrations in the park and elsewhere. On the night of 14 August there were searchlights, decorated yachts, bonfires and singing; and thousands danced on Poole Quay.

During the preceding six years the damage had amounted to sixty-seven civilians killed and over a hundred injured, eighty buildings destroyed and five thousand damaged.

Two ducks were killed by a bomb that fell in Poole Park. At the time a meeting was in progress in Parkstone Great Hall, which shook violently. But the roof stayed in place and the assembled officials and guests "burst out laughing".

In May two barrage balloons, sited near Poole Quay, were struck by lightning. The wires glowed with an intense white light and smoke, says a contemporary report. "Then the balloons caught fire and dropped flaming to the ground."

As far back as 1943 both national and local governments had begun to plan their post-war world. Poole Council wanted to widen the High Street and the destruction of several buildings by bombs offered the opportunity to make a start. It was not proposed deliberately to demolish more buildings but to carry out the widening piecemeal as they fell into decay or were removed by enemy action. But how short is human vision! No one could have foreseen that the High Street would be by-passed and become a quiet car-free lane, where people can do their shopping in peace and the loudest noise is the sound of their footsteps.

Poole, Christchurch and Bournemouth agreed that they should co-ordinate their post-war plans and Professor Patrick Abercrombie was invited to act as consultant. In March 1944 a town planning conference was held at Bournemouth and attended by Clough Williams Ellis and Elizabeth Scott, architect of the Shakespeare Memorial Theatre. Poole Chamber of Trade set up a development committee to consider the problems which businessmen would have to cope with after the war.

A Government White Paper at this time advised that post-war industrial development should be concentrated in the North East, South Wales and Lanarkshire. The conclusion drawn in Poole was that the Board of Trade would tend to veto industrial expansion in this area, as had happened in 1930 when the Ford Motor Company had wanted to build a factory at Hamworthy. They went instead to Dagenham. The White Paper was followed by the Distribution of Industry Bill and Poole's Special Development Commitee felt that it had been by-passed.

The new power station was being planned at an estimated cost of four million pounds, and property values reached an "all-time peak". At Lilliput a three-bedroom bungalow made headlines by fetching a price of £3,500, while another bungalow was reported to have been sold for £5,000.

During the next decades the foundations were laid of the Poole we know today. In April 1957 Mr Lionel Abbott, the district county planning officer, outlined to Poole Councillors his plan for the redevelopment of the town and the conservation of its old centre. In the years that followed the main lines of this plan were put into effect.

In 1958 it was announced that Poole Corporation would spend one million pounds on housing, sewerage, lighting and other public works. In the same year plans were published to reclaim the thirty acres of mudflats adjoining Baiter peninsula and extend the road towards Lilliput. The result is the grass-covered plateau which now adjoins Poole Park and provides the site for the Poole Boat Show, an annual event which soon expanded to include a variety of industries. Also in 1958 the plans for the new Civic Centre were announced.

Development to cost £50,000 was planned for Rockley Sands. Today Rockley with its caravan park and pleasant beaches is a self-contained holiday resort, offering every seaside recreation up in the landlocked harbour, and well-sheltered from sea storms.

During the 1960s the Corporation twice applied for County Borough status; but this development was prevented by the fact that the population

72

of the town was not large enough. County Borough status would have been quite distinct from that of "The Town and County of Poole" as established by the first Queen Elizabeth. But such matters are now academic, for within a few years the entire system of local government throughout the United Kingdom was to be reorganised, and Poole would in future be merely a district unit in the overall scheme. Obviously this has proved no hindrance to the vast developments of the past two decades.

Branksome Towers, etched by Newman and Company of London, about 1870. It was built in 1852, for H. Bury who created the basic road layout of Branksome Park and set the first spacious villas amid the pines. Here, according to 'Literary Dorset', crime writer Edgar Wallace wrote 'Mr Justice Maxell' in 1922. This superbly sited mansion, classic Victoriana, was demolished in 1973.

BOUNDLESS HORIZONS

THE MASSIVE complex of Poole's Civic Centre rises above the Municipal Buildings which were opened in 1931. The new blocks house the offices of those departments called into being by our modern Welfare State: Health and Social Security, Department of Employment, the Dorset Area Health Authority; also the Law Courts. The old Municipal Offices house the Council Chamber and the offices of Town Planning, Borough Engineer, Rates, Borough Treasurer and Town Clerk.

This administrative centre is outside what used to be the historic town of Poole which can be approached by three routes from the east side. Parkstone Road skirts the Park while to its right on higher ground Longfleet Road runs parallel and passes the splendidly modern General Hospital, opened in 1969 by her Majesty the Queen. To the right again, Wimborne Road is the third route leading into Poole. All converge in the area where the town gate used to be, and Towngate Street is nearby. Today the motorist can hardly be aware that he is crossing the neck of a peninsula. The water of the Poole Park lakes is screened from view, though sometimes the reedy fringe of Holes Bay to the right can be seen. The cluster of black-headed gulls standing there may expect scraps to descend upon them from the windows of offices and flats.

The converging traffic speeds on it way over a flyover underneath which passes the main railway line to the West and to London. On this border of the old town precincts the most conspicuous building is that of Barclay's International Bank. This consists of three massive circular blocks joined together like a clover leaf, while an overhead walkway links it with a multi-storey car park. These offices employ over four thousand people.

Once across the flyover, one is at liberty to pass straight down West Street and across Poole Bridge to Hamworthy and on into the heart of Dorset, or to fork left and find his way into the heart of the old town.

In West Street the various businesses enjoy ready access to deep water. The channel which passes along the quay, under Poole Bridge and then swings eastwards gives an average depth of ten feet at low water. Among the firms making use of this waterfront are Harveys, who run the harbour waterbuses and provide general services for yachtsmen. Harveys are among the oldest established watermen in the Poole area and it was one of their family who ferried the first Boy Scouts to Brownsea Island.

The internationally known name of Dalgety must be the first to catch the eye of the visitor as he makes his way along West Street towards the Quay. Until 1968 the name on this massive block was that of Christopher Hill, a historic one in the annals of Poole.

In 1846 the Hill family set themselves up as millers, using grain from local farms. The mill occupied the site where the Poole Aquarium now stands. The Christopher Hill Company took over several subsidiaries and specialised in animal feedstuffs. They moved to Castle Street and later to West Street.

In 1980 the company was taken over by Rank, Hovis, McDougall, by which time it was equipped with a mill controlled by computer and capable of blending and mixing sixty tonnes per hour.

In 1984 Christopher Hill became the Poole branch of Dalgety Agriculture Ltd. They run a distinctive fleet of yellow lorries with brown insignia.

Other prominent businesses along West Street are the builders' merchants Blanchard and Burgess and the factory and offices of British Drug Houses. On the inland side of the street stands the imposing new building of the Royal National Lifeboat Institution. Though square and functional, it has a pleasing appearance, the outline being softened by grey-brown curtain walling panels below the windows, the frames of which are thrust forward. The architect was Leslie Jones, and it was opened in 1976. The entire country-wide administrative apparatus of the Institution is accommodated here – records, appeals, technical research and many other departments. The Institution also owns a group of workshops on the other side of the road. Here the inshore rescue boats are laid up and a certain amount of maintenance done on the seagoing lifeboats.

Since 1983 the main Poole lifeboat has been the thirty-three feet Brede Class craft called *Inner Wheel*, the name deriving from the fact that the women's division of the Rotary Club were the chief contributors to its cost. It was built at Rye by Locklin Marine Ltd.

The RNLI also provides two twenty-one feet inshore rescue boats, the Boston whaler *Outrage* and the *Atlantic* semi-inflatable high-speed outboard boat.

Such craft make a striking contrast with the old lifeboat housed in a shed on the main quay as a historic relic. This old-timer, which took part in the Dunkirk evacuation of 1940, was nevertheless still doing a good job in the 1960s. Over the years Poole lifeboatmen have been awarded one gold and seven silver medals.

Anyone travelling along West Quay Road can hardly miss the imposing modern buildings bearing the name Sunseeker International. It occupies the site which was owned until a few years ago by Quay West Marina, and behind Sunseeker lies a remarkable and little-known success story.

In 1961 John and Robert Braithwaite started boatbuilding in a single shed at one end of the present premises. They now run a multi-million pound company specialising in high-powered motor cruisers and speedboats, some of the smallest of which may cost £27,000. Over 90 percent of production is exported. Evidently there is a brisk demand for the powerful, high-performance type of motor cruiser, as the company finds itself stretched to the limit to fulfill all its orders on time.

The service side of the business is expanding, but parking space is limited as the building side of it continues to expand. There are twenty-eight berths afloat and fresh water and electricity are accessible alongside.

On the opposite side of the town from West Street, several tall modern blocks of flats have arisen to transform Poole's skyline. Between these and West Street the heart of old Poole is to be found. It is a tribute to the blending of old and new that had been achieved that Poole was one of the four British towns chosen to represent this country in Europe Architectural Heritage Year 1975.

The historic buildings of the old town date from the two most notable periods in the commercial activity of Poole. Firstly, in the Middle Ages from the twelfth to the fifteenth centuries,when a considerable seaborne trade developed; and secondly during the eighteenth century, when the fisheries based on Newfoundland reached their peak. The first period produced such buildings as Scaplen's Court and the Town Cellars. The eighteenth century gave rise to the splendid mansions of the shipowners and the more modest homes of such people as ship's masters and mates, whose dwellings may be seen in the terraced houses of Church Street and Market Street. But the fishery and the great houses declined and parts of the old town became a collection of unsavoury dwellings falling ever further into decay. It would have been easy to demolish all but the best of them and start afresh. But the Borough Council decided to designate a whole area for conservation, including shops, light industry and quite ordinary houses. In 1964 a survey of the proposed conservation area was made and a year later the Council outlined the measures they proposed to put into effect. In some cases property was bought, in others mortgages were arranged to enable the occupants to carry out renovations.

The plans for the renewal of Poole's historic past as represented in brick and stone included the conversion of the one-time Town Cellars into a maritime museum. This building was known in Tudor times as the "Wool House" – nearby Blandford was in those days one of the most important towns in England due to its situation in the heart of the sheep-raising country. The walls of this building are of Purbeck stone and date from about 1430. The present museum, which extends into the adjoining eighteenth century warehouse, includes among its exhibits the first X-class yacht, built in 1909, and features describing our naval history, such as the press gangs, the Newfoundland fisheries, smuggling and the Revenue men; and a display of the wild flowers to be found around the harbour shores.

On the quayside, where Thames Street meets the Quay, is the Customs House, built in 1813 in late Georgian style. In front of it stands a heavily-built wooden T-shaped cross known as the Town Beam. It is eleven feet high and has an iron ring at the end of each arm, and was used for weighing merchandise. It bears a plaque inscribed with the following extract from Poole Corporation records for 1579: "The Baylye or his Deputye shall receive of every stranger or ffarinor having goodes or marchandyzes to be wayed, for the paysadze or weighinge the same at the

Towne Beame appointed for that purpose, one half-pennye for every hundred weight, which half pennye shall be the whole duty as well for the Beame as for the porters and labour for the puttinge in and taking out."

A few minutes' walk away from the Quay stands one of Poole's most historic buildings, Scaplen's Court. It may have been the earliest seat of local government and later became the home of Sheriff John Scaplen. The story of the rediscovery and restoration of this building began in 1924 when the collapse of a chimney stack through the roof led to an investigation by the historian H.P. Smith. At that time it was divided into six tenements in which that number of families lived. The building was restored through the joint efforts of the Society of Poole Men and the Corporation, but after being open to the public for twenty-one years it had to be closed owing to structural decay. Under the direction of the Borough Engineer it was gradually restored, and reopened in 1959.

Notable features of Scaplen's Court are the Upper Hall, with a fine fifteenth century collar-beam roof, oriel window and oak wainscot. A loft at one end may have been used by travelling minstrels.

The suite used by the master of the house is known as the 'Solar', and here again is a fine example of the collar-beam roof. Above the fireplace a doorway, now blocked, used to give access to the attics. Some interesting features of the Lower Hall also remain. It used to have a huge open fireplace, beautiful oriel window, green tiles and oak-panelled walls.

Scaplen's Court is also interesting as a museum. The exhibits include pottery from the early Iron Age, wheat grains and oats in a small pot which was found in a clay-lined pit near Corfe Mullen and dated between 50 BC and AD 50. The ancient canoe recovered from the harbour has been mentioned in Chapter One. Also of local interest is the iron casting of Leonardo's picture *The Last Supper*, made at Waterloo Foundry, Poole by a Mr Palmer. This won first prize in the Iron Section at the Great Exhibition at Crystal Palace in 1851.

Several historic buildings are thus grouped around the point where Thames Street meets Sarum Street, just a few yards off the Quay. Thames Street leads to St James Church, the parish church of Poole. It was built in 1819 on the site of an earlier church which fell into ruin. It is an attractive church with pleasing light effects, tall piers of Oregon pine from Newfoundland and a fine reredos in Spanish mahogany. In the time of Edward IV a south aisle was added and a north aisle about 1500. In 1406 it was damaged by an invading force of French and Spaniards who came to avenge the damage caused by Harry Paye, the famous or infamous Poole pirate. Henry VIII made the church a "Royal Peculiar", as a result of which the choir has the privilege of wearing scarlet cassocks.

St James had a good collection of Holy Communion plates. One of its parish clerks was William Knapp, who in 1738 and 1753 published volumes of hymns and anthems. Best known is his hymn entitled "Wareham", named after the town of his birth. In the graveyard is the grave of the successful merchant James Thompson, who directed that his body should be placed in a wooden coffin treated with pitch, filled with spirits of wine and sealed. This coffin was then placed inside another made of lead, which was placed in yet a third coffin, handsomely carved out of wood. All this was then placed in a stone sarcophagus in the family vault.

It was in the seventeenth century that a Rector named Hancock denounced the Roman Catholic hierarchy and called the Host "that Jack-in-the-box". The medal awarded to Peter Joliffe in 1694 has been mentioned; one of his descendants, P.W.Joliffe, was Rector of St James from 1792 to 1861 and died the oldest clergyman in Britain aged over ninety.

The Alms Houses of St George are in nearby Church Street; the commemorative plaque above the entrance tells us that the houses were built in the reign of Henry V and were bought by Poole Corporation in 1550. They have been devoted to the accommodation of the poor for 500 years.

A few minutes' walk from St James Church is the old Guildhall, an attractive Georgian building dating from 1761. Crescent-shaped stone stairways lead up on either side to the portico entrance on the first floor. The Town Council used to meet here until the completion of the new municipal buildings at Park Gates in 1932. This picturesque eighteenth century hall, built of red brick with white stone quoins and keystones, had begun to deteriorate badly when in 1971 the Corporation undertook the task of restoring and maintaining it. Now it is a museum and the first exhibit a visitor will notice is an eighteenth century fire engine. It consists of a hand pump with leather hosepipe mounted on a trolley. It is surprising to learn from the descriptive notice that this kind of apparatus was in use in some Dorset villages in 1940 for fighting hedge fires. Other exhibits include Poole pottery, antique coins and some remarkable historic gramophones and clocks.

Near the Guildhall is Guildhall Court, a row of flats built in 1969 in a style which harmonises with the Georgian without being merely a copy. At the same time one side of Market Street was closed to traffic, thus preventing the Guildhall from becoming an island with cars revolving round it. These flats and a block in New Orchard gained an award for good design from the Department of the Environment.

Developments in Thames Street and Cinnamon Lane are other examples of the blending of new with old. In both cases a jumble of old houses and commercial premises, many in a state of decay, was tidied up and modernised or restored. The restoration of the Guildhall, the flats in Cinnamon Lane and New Orchard and Cinnamon Court were the work of the Architect's Department of Poole Council headed by Mr G. Hopkinson. The houses in Thames Street were designed by Mr John King of Arlington Developments Ltd.

These developments won the approval of Sir John Betjeman, but not everybody took a favourable view of them. The author of a study of Poole's commercial development in 1968 stigmatised the Council's plans to concentrate industry on the Nuffield Estate as 'Utopian', and he thought the creation of the Arndale Centre would "cut the town in half". One section of the population would patronise the Arndale while on the other side of the town there would be empty car parks. If only there were some half-empty ones!

The Arndale Centre, on the western fringe of the town, typifies the most modern aspect of development in the ancient seaport. Besides housing spacious branches of such well-known stores as Sainsbury, Boots and Marks and Spencer, the Arndale includes a sports centre where there are facilities for squash, archery, badminton, table tennis, judo and karate.

Here also is the modern lending library and reference library, with its historic local newspapers on microfilm, and store-room with its wealth of historic documents. These are still in process of being catalogued. Before his resignation Mr Leonard J. Shaw had compiled four volumes of the calendar of archives.

A few yards away across the road stands an even more recent addition to Poole's new buildings, the Arts Centre. This rather functional modern building is the realisation of the dreams of all those who have hoped and planned for better provision for artistic endeavour every since Victorian times. The new block was completed in 1978 and comprises a concert hall which can seat 1,500 – as many as the Bournemouth Pavilion – and a 600-seat theatre, the Towngate Theatre, with a stage measuring thirty-five by thirty-three feet. The auditorium is steeply raked so that nobody's view is blocked by the person in front, and the lighting and the dressing rooms are of a standard which must be the envy of all but the best-equipped theatres in the country. As to the concert hall, its auditorium can be transformed into a flat floor for dances or exhibitions at the touch of a switch.

The Dorset Room is for gatherings of up to a hundred. Arts and crafts exhibitions are held in the Canford Room and Longfleet Gallery. The Branksea Restaurant seats a hundred and twenty, and advertises "superb cuisine". It can produce up to six hundred meals for banquets in the Wessex Hall from "superbly equipped kitchens". For a country suffering from inflation and economic crisis in the 1970s, this Arts Centre is an astonishing assertion of prosperity and idealism. Caught in the inflationary tide after building had started, its cost rose to four-and-a-half million pounds.

Such flowerings of the arts spring from the wealth created by commerce, and even a superficial glance around Poole must impress the observer with the number of new factories and workshops on its outskirts.

The great expansion of industry in the post-war period has been concentrated in two adjacent areas: the Nuffield Estate and Fleet's Lane which borders Holes Bay. Some of the massive business premises which may catch the eye of the passing motorist are those of Dolphin Packaging, the DIY Super Centre, Atholl Ltd.,specialists in heating and air conditioning, and Aish and Co., electrical engineers.

The Nuffield Industrial Estate is some two miles from the centre of Poole town and only the Fleet's Bridge flyover separates it from the Fleet's Lane factory belt. The biggest company to be found here is Hamworthy Engineering, which is probably the biggest industrial company in the Poole-Bournemouth area and is made up of five divisions. These produce pumps and compressors mainly for marine use, combustion equipment, hydraulic apparatus and transmission systems, while the foundry manufactures castings. Some sixty percent of production is exported. Hamworthy Engineering is a part of the Powell Dufferyn Group.

The bias of modern Poole is towards engineering and manufactures based on metal. It is indeed a long way from the fishing fleet and the potteries of old. Among the enterprises prominent on the Nuffield Estate the visitor may notice the B & Q Autocentre, Southern Toolmaking, Hunt's Motorists' Centre, Marley Tiles and Palm Circuits Ltd. Among this hive of enterprise is the firm J & S Sieger who manufacture gas detectors and alarms. The company was started in 1959 by Joshua Sieger with three assistants. It now employs three hundred people and has won two National Export Awards.

Not such a happy story is that of British Seagull which grew from a back street in Poole to a modern factory on the Ringwood road to which it moved in the late 1970s, only to fall victim to Japanese and American competition.

The extent of Poole's shore-based industry is shown by the number of different firms listed in 1978: Engineering 140; Electrical/Automation 50; Yacht and Boatbuilding and all associated trades 73; Road Haulage Contractors 25; Printers, Engravers, Publishers 32; Food, Confectionery etc. 17; Joinery, Timber etc.30; Pottery, Bricks, Tiles, Glass, Concrete 16. The list of miscellaneous companies totals one hundred and includes such names at Bluebird Caravans, Metal Box, Remploy, Ryvita, Plessey and Marley Tiles.

Shipbuilding has dwindled to nothing in recent years, but yachts and small boats are still built in several yards around the harbour. In 1957 Bolsons launched a steel raft one hundred and forty feet long and forty feet wide. The Dutch took on the task of towing this unwieldly burden five thousand miles to Lake Maracaibo to be used in drilling for oil. In 1956 R.A.Newman launched a ninety feet motor yacht, believed to be the biggest private yacht to be built at Poole. However Newman's yard on Poole Quay has been taken over by Southern Ocean Supplies who built the Ocean 75 sailing yacht. This is the world's largest glassfibre yacht in series production, and in 1977 the price was £300,000. It is being followed by the Ocean 90, priced at £750,000.

Just down the harbour coastline from Poole Park, F.C.Mitchell has a fifty-year old waterside boatbuilding business. In 1976 their exports totalled £200,000 and went to countries all over the world, including the United States, Australia and Africa. One of their products is the locally well-known 'Brownsea' cruiser class.

Dorset Lake Shipyard, one-and-a-quarter miles along the Hamworthy shore from Poole quays, offers every facility for the yachtsman and in the past has built minesweepers of three hundred and sixty tons. This company has also handled the maintenance of the US landing craft which were moored in a long line bordering the Wareham Channel soon after the last war until 1977.

Here again the building of large ships has been abandoned but Rotork Marine Ltd., a divison of a multi-national company, have acquired the main shed and a large part of the waterfront, and here they build a large range of workboats up to a length of forty-one feet. All Rotork craft are built of reinforced polyester and basically resemble landing craft with their shallow draught and rectangular hulls. The makers call them sea-trucks and these practical boats are used as lifeboats, fireboats, ferries and for surveying, fishery protection, weed-cutting and many other purposes. Many are exported.

The great majority of shipping and forwarding agents in Poole give their address as The Ferry Terminal, Hamworthy. This means that their business is with the Truckline Service which carries laden lorries between Poole and Cherbourg. Truckline has been the most dramatic development in the seaborne trade of Poole since the great Newfoundland fishery dwindled into insignificance about a hundred and fifty years ago. It was inaugurated in 1973, a special terminal having been created for it on reclaimed land. The impact of Truckline can be seen in the figures provided by Poole Harbour Commissioners: In 1972 foreign trade in and out of Poole totalled in value £12,992,950. In 1975 this figure was £213,647,887. Since then a second Truckline terminal has been constructed complete with parking space and there are four sailings a day in each direction. Truckline are considering the extension of their summertime passenger service which started on a weekly basis between Poole and its twin town, Cherbourg. The ownership of Truckline passed to Brittany Ferries in 1985.

The cross-Channel journey takes four-and-a-half hours and the turn-round time is two-and-a-half hours. There is room in the parking area for two hundred and eighty vehicles and both trailers and driver-accompanied vehicles are taken on board. *Coutances* and *Purbeck* each carry forty trailers and a hundred motor cars. Some 30,000 Citroen cars are brought in yearly. Truckline has raised Poole to twenty-sixth place among UK ports from sixty first in 1969. And all because somebody realised it was possible to design a ship of 3,000 tons and capable of carrying over 1,000 tons of cargo which still only draws eleven feet. The depth on the harbour bar and near Poole Quay drops to twelve feet at low water – and these ships which tower like monsters over the coastal lowlands nose their way to their terminal even at low water.

The Truckline service now attracts cargoes from all over the country. On the outskirts of the town may be seen signposts inscribed 'Ro-Ro'. In this poetic fashion the heavy lorry driver is directed towards the roll-on, roll-off service to Cherbourg and, he may hope, a smooth crossing. The wish is not always granted, and when the *Vechstroom*, a replacement for the *Dorset* made her first crossing on 9 January 1978 several lorries were thrown on to their sides in a force nine gale. Bottles of wine were broken; but if the decks ran red at least it was not with blood, as it well might have been in earlier centuries.

Fish, meat, chemicals and "groupage loads" are exported. Imports include Zanussi electrical appliances, mixed loads, fruit and vegetables, wines and car spares.

Poole's traditional seaborne trade serves an area within a radius of about fifty miles for cargoes of imported grain, timber, sea-dredged sand and gravel and fertilisers, while imported steel is distributed all over the South and Midlands. There are plans to expand the port's wharfage capacity north of the power station and along the Hamworthy shoreline. Poole now handles 300,000 tonnes of petrol and petroleum products every year.

In 1978 the estimated population of Poole was 117,000. Among the industrialists who established themselves here not a few were strongly influenced by the beauty of the surrounding country and its facilities for recreation. This was true of George Jennings, who founded the South Western Pottery in 1856. Firstly there is the harbour with its great expanse of protected water. Beyond lies the attractive and varied Dorset coast to the west and fourteen miles to the eastward, the Solent and the Isle of Wight. For those who do not go afloat there is all the beauty of Hampshire and Dorset at one's back door.

Curiously contradictory statements have been published regarding the actual area of Poole Harbour. The length of its entire coastline is commonly said to be ninety-nine miles. But Rodney Legg, whose book *Purbeck Island* is perhaps the most comprehensive work about this district, reckons it is about fifty-two miles round. I am sure that the figure of ninety-nine, so firmly embedded in local folklore, is wildly exaggerated and it would be interesting to know how it originated. Even by tracing the coastline up and down every muddy creek the total mileage cannot be stretched to this extent.

Whatever the acreage, what is certain is that the pressure of population and the power of the petrol engine have reduced the great harbour to an extension of Poole Park – a large boating lake which the Commissioners have had to protect from proliferating speedboats by designating "quiet areas" over much of the harbour's western side. Here there is a speed limit of six knots. Harvey's Water Buses promenade around the harbour like sedate, glass-fronted swans. Yet on this domesticated lake in former ages great ships have been wrecked and pirates engaged in a breathtaking chase to their hide-outs.

A dozen yacht clubs cater for the ever-increasing boating activity, ten of them situated on the eastern borders of the harbour. Cobb's Quay, founded about 1935 by Mr W.E.Cobb, is the most remote of them. To reach it, the yachtsman has to pass under Poole bridge and weave through moorings and narrow channels, at the end of which he finds the thirty-acre complex of yards, chandlery and engineering shops and a marina capable of accommodating seven hundred yachts, while five hundred and fifty can be laid-up ashore. There is also a clubhouse and restaurant and showers; and a residential building for visitors is planned. The yard can handle vessels of up to one hundred tons.

Not far along the Hamworthy shore is Poole Yacht Club, a stronghold of sailing men with the emphasis on cruising rather than dinghies. The devotees of racing catamarans have found a base here, having previously been based on the Lilliput Sailing Club, and before that the Parkstone Yacht Club. Laying-up space at Poole Yacht Club is limited, but they have about two hundred and fifty moorings adjacent to the Wareham Channel.

Some two miles further west and we are at Rockley Point and the entrance to Lychett Bay, spanned by the bridge across which the intrepid local reporter made the first crossing by train in 1846. On the headland is a caravan park and below it a sailing school and every kind of facility to do with enjoying oneself afloat or on the beach in delightfully sheltered waters. Also at Hamworthy is the Poole Harbour Commissioners Boat Haven, with three hundred and fifty berths afloat.

The remaining clubs are situated at intervals along the east and south-east shores of the harbour. The Parkstone is the largest with about two thousand members and an extensive dinghy park, boatyards and work-shops. There is a waiting list for membership. The club was founded in 1895 as the Parkstone Boating and Pier Club. Exactly how many members there were is not known, but the income from subscriptions in 1897 was £32 and insurance cost 11s.3d.

For several years Parkstone Yacht Club has been the sponsor of Poole Yachting Week which in 1977 attracted four hundred and seventy-nine entries. In fact this event has become so popular that the number of participants has had to be limited. The recently extended lounge and the spacious terrace outside give a magnificent view of the harbour and the Purbeck Hills.

About half-a-mile further south the Lilliput Sailing Club, founded in 1956, stands on the edge of Parkstone Lagoon, a tidal basin with a narrow entrance. At low tide the acres of mud are most attractive to waterfowl, less so the yachtsmen. However the lagoon does afford as sheltered water as may be found anywhere in the harbour.

Lilliput Sailing Club has many keen sailing members, as its name implies, and its total membership is around six hundred. Its one hundred or so moorings are all booked, and so is the available space for the winter lay-up. Members have access to the adjacent Blue Lagoon Restaurant.

Outside Parkstone Lagoon, less than half-a-mile away, is Poole Harbour Yacht Club, which was founded in the 1930s and was always strong on the social side. In recent years under the aegis of the Salterns Way Club it has blossomed forth to an extent not always appreciated by its neighbours. Land had been reclaimed and blocks of luxury flats tower over the Lagoon, while at the end of the promontory which juts out towards the main harbour channel another large building has appeared, though not a high one. This houses the Marina offices and those of the yacht builders and brokers Marine Secol, Moody and Sadler. At the chandleries, which include Piplers, the yachtsmen can obtain anything from a sun hat to a sailboard, and get lessons in how to sail it too.

At the landward end of the Marina is a two thousand square feet boatshed, and workshops capable of handling both engineering and woodwork.

The Marina has two hundred and fifty berths alongside pontoons and there are seventy-five offshore moorings. The berths can accommodate craft up to sixty feet length and eight feet draught. Charges range from £1,198 per year for an eight-metre yacht to £2,750 for one of eighteen metres. Smaller boats are able to enter the section of the Marina nearest to the shore and for them the fees are proportionately lower.

The club offers well-furnished amenities plus a squash court. It is amalgamated with Salterns Hotel, recently modernised. Conferences of up to a hundred delegates can be accommodated.

Following our southward course along the shore we arrive at Lilliput Yacht Station, presided over by Mr Royston Pizey. Moorings, laying-up and the other usual facilities are provided, but space is limited.

A few hundred yards further on we are at the foot of Evening Hill where an unpretentious little red brick block proclaims itself to be the home of the East Dorset Sailing Club. It has eighty full members and one hundred 'pier' members. Maybe it is no great disadvantage to be a pier member, since the modest clubhouse offers few facilities and no bar. But it does have a useful pier, leading across Whitley Lake towards the main channel. When they first built the pier they were ordered to remove it forthwith or pay an annual rent of £1. They had committed an illegal act on a part of Lord Wimborne's estates.

A wide, shallow bay stretches from this point to the cluster of shops at Sandbanks. It is here that the newest of the yacht and boat clubs has established itself, the North Haven Lake Association. In recent years the bay has become the playground of boardsailers, who perhaps prefer the more romantic name of windsurfers. With an average depth of around five feet at high water, this area is ideal for the sport, especially if you are a beginner, and on any summer day its exponents can be seen speeding in all directions like a flock of multi-coloured butterflies.

Less than half-a-mile away, across the neck of Sandbanks, is another favourite take-off point for boardsailers. This is the open sea, but even in midwinter and in gale force winds the experts almost fly at twenty knots out to the rollers on Hook Sands and indeed from time to time go airborne off the crest of a wave.

Sandbanks has the Royal Motor Yacht Club which was founded in 1905 by the Royal Automobile Club. Its position is unsurpassed as it commands a splendid view of the harbour. As its name suggests, the RMYC is the chief base for motor cruisers, but its membership of 1,400 includes many keen sailing men and women.

This club was responsible for establishing the X Class, remarkable not only for sailing ability but also for the way it has withstood the test of time since its creation on the Isle of Wight in 1909.

The RMYC started in a yacht at Southampton and moved to Poole through its amalgamation with the British Motor Boat Club. The clubhouse was a yacht named *Florinda*, moored alongside Poole Quay. In 1935 the clubhouse at Sandbanks was built with seventeen 'cabins' offering modern comfort. Since 1952 the Duke of Edinburgh has been the Club's 'Admiral'.

All these yacht clubs provide moorings and laying-up space; so do boatyards such as Harvey's, Mitchell's and the Lilliput Yacht Station. But nowadays the yachtsman has learned the advantages of berthing in a marina. Failing this device, the visiting yachtsman must anchor and use his dinghy, find a temporary mooring or jostle against other yachts at a crowded quayside. An artificial yacht-harbour, known nowadays as a marina, provides a network of pontoons connected to a central walkway. The yachtsman pulls in beside a pontoon, ties up and walks ashore without further ado. Most marinas provide showers: some also offer a restaurant and accommodation.

The existing marinas at Cobb's Quay and Lilliput are far from adequate for the needs of Poole, where in 1966 an aerial photograph revealed some six thousand boats afloat.

To meet their needs the Poole District Plan includes a scheme which would involve the reclamation of a further thirty-four acres of mudflats adjoining Baiter peninsula. Along the coastline towards the Parkstone Yacht Club, yachtsmen would be provided with "boat-haven/alongside facilities" and some building development is envisaged. Opinion among residents in the neighbourhood is by no means unanimously in favour of these projects.

At Sandbanks we come to the end of the urbanised or suburbanised side of the harbour and from North Haven Point may gaze across to the heathlands and the hills. But now there is a difference; for hidden among the scrub and the heather is the Wytch Farm oilfield and from time to time a drilling rig sprouts from the heath as new reservoirs of oil are discovered. The first borehole at Wytch Farm was sunk in 1975 and it is said the owner offered the oilmen a thousand pounds to go away. But Mr Pitman is now reconciled to the upheaval and the compensation. The Ryder family who own the land have also had to accept the inevitable with good grace. The local representatives of the nature conservation societies have made their views felt and where digging is done the soil is removed layer by layer and put back as it was, to the benefit of the sand lizard and the smooth snake.

British Petroleum took over the operation of Wytch Farm in 1985. Two reservoirs known as Bridport Sands and Sherwood Sands are in process of development and are expected to yield 40,000 barrels a day. The expansion of the oil industry entails the laying of new pipelines and a corresponding expansion of the Rail Loading Terminal at Furzebrook, near Wareham. The expanded Wytch field is expected to yield 60,000 barrels a day.

Having come to the end of this brief survey of Poole's history, what strikes one most forcibly is the vast and dramatic transformation which has taken place during the last thirty years. Up to the end of the last war, there were still traces of remoteness, the separateness that had characterised Poole through the centuries. Commercially its record has been patchy. The shallow nature of the harbour had always limited the development of seaborne trade. Then suddenly all is high blocks of flats, trunk roads and new companies by the dozen, the ceaseless traffic to and from Cherbourg and a population of over a hundred thousand.

Cynics have said that our part of the country is now merely an outer suburb of London, say SW 504. If the world is becoming a "global village" still more is England becoming one large suburb. Nevertheless regions and towns as yet retain their individual character. The Dorset speech is still to be heard, distinct from that of its neighbours in Somerset and Devon. Nowadays conservation is a watchword to be heard on all sides. There are still beautiful, even wild, places on our doorstep, and the majority of people are better off than at any previous period in history.

St Peter's church and schools, Parkstone, engraved by Philip Brannon, about 1860. They were built in 1833-34 and the church would be partially rebuilt in 1876. The riders are in St Peter's Road and the view is northward from Parr Street.

Poole Cemetery, drawn by Philip Brannon, about 1860. The elaborate entrance faces Cemetery Avenue which branches off Ringwood Road and crosses Dorchester Road.

SOME SOURCES

Acts of the Privy Council 20 October 1577. Public Records Office.
A Cruising Voyage Round the World by Woodes Rogers. Preface by G.F.Mainwaring 1928.
Alfred the Great and his England by Eleanor Duckett. Collins 1957.
BP Public Relations Office. Calendar of Archives. Poole Reference Library.
Commercial Directories.
Dorset by John Hyams.
Dorset Elizabethans by Rachel Lloyd.
Dorset Harbours by Donald Payne.
The Defeat of the Spanish Armada by Garrett Mattingley.
The Anglo-Saxon Chronicle, translated by H.N. Garmonsway 1955.
History of Poole by H.P.Smith, published 1948/51.
History of Poole by J.Sydenham, published 1839.
History of Poole by Bernard Short, 1932.
The Later History of Poole by Bernard Short, 1932.
I Call to Mind by Herbert Carter.
Life of King Alfred. Asser, Ed. W.H.Stevenson 1904.
Oyer and Terminer Records, H.C.A.1, 1535-1834. Trials of Pirates, Public Records Office.
Life of Philip Henry Gosse by Edmund Gosse.
Port of Poole 1977, issued by Poole Harbour Commissioners.
Poole Pottery, report issued by the company.
Pike, Dorset Suits Vol 5. Arundel v. Stourton, A3/59, 22 Jan. 1595. County Museum, Dorchester.
Poole and the Armada, Catholic Record Society Vol 21/119.
Poole and Dorset Herald. Poole Reference Library.
Poole and Newfoundland by F.W.Matthews, Poole and Parkstone Standard 1936.

Index

Canford

Canford House, about 1850. Canford's lands extended across Parkstone and Poole to the sea – hence the placename Canford Cliffs. It provided the lord of the manor. At the time of this cricket match the estate was owned by steel magnate Sir John Josiah Guest, who had bought it from W.F.S. Ponsonby, first Baron de Mauley, in 1845. Canford House became Canford School in 1923 and its former Canford Magna parish is now part of Poole.

Poole seal, 1300s. The artistic exaggeration, showing the colossal 'castles' fore and aft, highlight a problem with galleon design – designer instability – that would sink Henry VIII's 'Mary Rose' with all hands, as she sailed out of Portsmouth towards Spithead in 1545.

Poole Quay

Poole Bridge, about 1900. Seen from the Hamworthy side of the water, with a full line of ships, double-moored in places, along the western length of Poole Quay. On the quayside there was some activity and at least one traction engine and a railway waggon can be glimpsed.

OPPOSITE, top
Poole Quay, about 1905. A full line-up of ships along the Quay, which is seen from the Hamworthy side of the water. Here the yachts are berthed, starting with the newest and smallest, 'White Kitten'.

OPPOSITE
Poole Quay, about 1908. Timber being carried in the foreground, with a convoy of horse-drawn waggons, loaded with bags of coal, moving past the grain warehouse. This view is looking eastward from the bridge.

Poole Quay. No 9.

Poole Quay, about 1910. Eastwards from the Custom House (left) showing the rail tracks running towards the overhead gantry which lifted coal into the gas works.

Poole Quay, about 1910. Another view looking east, on a rather quiet day.

Boat building, Poole, about 1920. The traditional methods of an ancient craft, still practised in the yards at West Quay and Hamworthy, which now generally manufacture fibreglass yachts and launches.

Poole Bridge. This metal structure, erected in 1885, was being replaced in 1927. Seen from Poole Quay, with demolition in progress on the Hamworthy side of the water. The Poole Harbour Board notice reads: 'No Goods, Carts or Vehicles of any description are allowed to remain on the Quays after Working Hours, under a Penalty of £5. H.W. Chislett, Harbour Master.'

Poole Quay, 1945. Pennants flying for Victory in Europe Day, the official moment being 15.00 hours on Thursday 8 May. These gunboats had already been stood down; their barrels have been removed. The view is from the vicinity of the Custom House, with the north-eastern extremity of Lower Hamworthy visible on the other side of the Quay Channel.

Poole Quay and Lower Hamworthy, about 1960. Seen from the east with the Lifeboat Station being the first building immediately on the nearside shore. Behind are the Gas Works coal heaps and gantries. Poole Quay is in the middle distance with the Old Town to its right, around St James's church. Across the Back Water Channel is Hamworthy Power Station. Lower Hamworthy extends to the left.

OPPOSITE
Moored off Poole, 1946-47. British Airways engine inspection for a former Royal Air Force Sunderland flying boat, its gun turret (in the bow) removed. Operating from Poole, the aircraft flew the long-distance Empire routes to Africa, India, the Far East and Australia.

Poole Bridge, 1960s. Opening time for Poole's third bridge, built in 1927 at a cost of £50,000 and lifted by electric power. A fishing boat is passing through. Each cabin carries Poole's borough arms in Della Robia ware. The view is from The Quay and in the background are the timber warehouses of J.T. Sydenham Limited.

OPPOSITE

Town Cellars or the Woolhouse, 1960s. Dating from about the 1430s, this outstanding mediaeval roof now covers the town's Maritime Museum. It was built beside the Quay as a wool store, probably shortly after Poole became a Port of the Staple, which was in 1433. Staple commodities were those upon which customs duty was levied and their merchandising was restricted by law to approved traders.

Custom House, Poole Quay, 1969. The impressive 1813 frontage is a replica of an earlier Georgian building that was destroyed by fire. Beside it, the Staplecross is a copy of that which would have been erected when Poole became a Port of Staple in 1433. It is also called the Town Beam.

OPPOSITE
Town Cellars and Providence (or Paradise) Street, early 1970s. Showing the Tudor stone-built single storey barn of a warehouse and the six floors of its brick-built early nineteenth century counterpart. The buildings were earmarked for the town's Maritime Museum. The left-hand brick wall, with the poster hoardings for Cydrex, Haig and Wondermash, was built when Thames Street was literally cut through the centre section of the mediaeval Town Cellars. The street was extended through the building, to open on to the Quay, in the late eighteenth century.

The Jolly Sailor Inn, Poole Quay, 1970s. Edwardian green-glazed bricks make this an unusual frontage. They were manufactured by Carter and Company, who then owned the nearby Poole Pottery. The picture was taken on a thirsty afternoon before the relaxation of licensing hours.

Hamworthy

Hamworthy and Holes Bay, 1949. In-flight refuelling of a Royal Air Force Meteor by a Lancaster tanker. Later that year the procedure enabled the RAF to claim the international endurance record for a jet fighter's range. Meanwhile, in the ground between the Meteor and the mud-flats, Hamworthy Power Station was taking shape. In the distance, Branksome Park lies beneath the tanker and Sandbanks is below the fighter.

Hamworthy, 1960s. Ship-repair on one of the slips opposite Poole Quay.

OPPOSITE
Lower Hamworthy, 1959. Beached hulks of the Solent-class flying boats, 'City of Liverpool' (right) and 'Solway', that had been left to float in Poole Harbour when British Overseas Airways moved its operations to Hythe, Southampton Water, in 1948.

Hamworthy Quay, 1964. Locomotive No.2, 'Western Pride' was the last steam engine to work the sidings and tramways at Hamworthy. She was scrapped but her sister saddle tank, No.1, 'Bonnie Prince Charlie' has been preserved in the collection at Didcot, Oxfordshire.

Lower Hamworthy, 1972. The railway lines continue past the former Hamworthy Station to the quays at Lower Hamworthy. Sidings to the left lead to Corralls' fuel tanks.

Hamworthy Station, 1972. This was Poole's first railway station, and its only one from the inauguration of the service on 1 May 1847 until 1872. The line from Southampton to Dorchester then snaked inland via Ringwood and Wimborne. Its two mile siding down the Hamworthy peninsula branched off at Hamworthy Junction. From there the line then went north in a wide curve across Upton Heath.

Hamworthy and Holes Bay, about 1980. Compare this with the similar aerial view featuring the refuelling Meteor. There are huge changes. Not only is Hamworthy Power Station a major landmark, but there is a marina between the saltings, major development on the opposite shore, and a vast area reclaimed from the harbour at Lower Hamworthy (towards the top right). Numerous faint white specks represent more than a thousand yachts.

OPPOSITE
Poole boat, 1980s. 'Environist' heading out to sea, with the sleek lines of the late twentieth century cabin cruiser. The mast assembly is capped by a radar scanner. Twin funnels aft keep engine exhaust clear of the deck. She was designed by Sandy Balfour of Coastal Ship Designs and built by Berthon Boat Limited.

Lower Hamworthy and Poole Quay, 1980s. Truckline ferry berthing at the container depot, with a timber ship outward bound. Tower blocks noticeable around the Old Town with the most conspicuous building (upper right) being Barclays House at the south end of Wimborne Road.

Bourne Valley

Surrey Road, Bourne Valley, 1884. The new permanent way from Bournemouth to Poole would be across the viaduct. This is the westward of the two over Surrey Road, and the first to be built; the other would go to a new Bournemouth West station at Westbourne. The house, beside which is a steam traction engine, is in Surrey Road. The photographer was standing in what is now Gordon Road. The rails, worked by a tank engine, form a temporary construction way which was later lifted.

OPPOSITE, top

High Street, Poole [north end], about 1900. Looking towards Longfleet from the pavement outside the Port Mahon Castle Hotel, before the laying of tram lines.

OPPOSITE

High Street, Poole [north end], 1914. Relaying the tramlines beside the Port Mahon Castle Hotel (centre right) which carries the name of the Poole-based Marston's Dolphin Brewery Limited on its gable wall. Note that the tracks did not follow the High Street, which bends left after Jordan's sign — because of the level crossing the tram system was never extended into the Old Town.

High Street, Poole

Tram Terminus.

High Street, Poole [north end], about 1915. The tram terminus was outside Davis the tobacconist and the Port Mahon Castle Hotel at the Longfleet Road end of the High Street. In 1905, Poole's rails joined the Bournemouth network and it would have been possible to board this tram (No.12) and travel via The Square to Christchurch; a journey of one-and-a-half hours for a fare of ninepence.

High Street, Poole [northern section], about 1910. Closed gates at the level crossing. With the construction of the railway to Bournemouth West in 1874, the Old Town peninsula had this as its only access until the building of the Towngate flyover in the 1960s.

POOLE: RAILWAY GATES, HIGH STREET. 41437.

High Street, Poole [north central part], in the 1950s. The view south, with bicycles almost outnumbering the cars. Butler's house furnishers are on the left corner, and the Gas Board showrooms opposite.

High Street, Poole [central part], about 1905. The cottage was already an anachronism and a favourite with Edwardian postcard producers: 'This Old Thatched Cottage in the Centre of High Street, Poole, supposed to be built in the year 1308 AD'. It stood on the west side of the High Street, immediately north of its junction with Carter's Lane (seen straight ahead, leading to Hill Street). Demolition took place in 1919, for Woolworth's Penny Bazaar, and on the site now is a pizza house.

Gasworks, Emerson Road, 1970s. An overhead railway carried ship-borne coal from the eastern end of Poole Quay to this major complex between Emerson Road and the railway. It became redundant with the piping of natural gas from the North Sea but some of the buildings resisted demolition.

OPPOSITE

Poole Station, 23 May 1960. Arrival from Waterloo of 1945-built 4-6-2 Merchant Navy class locomotive 35018 'British India Line'. Britain's last mainline steam trains ran from London to Weymouth until 1967 when the line was electrified to Bournemouth and diesel units continued to the west.

Poole Arts Centre

Poole Arts Centre, Kingland Road, 23 March 1979. Her Majesty Queen Elizabeth II and the Duke of Edinburgh (far left) meeting members of the Bournemouth Symphony Orchestra.

Old Town, Poole

Market Street and the Guildhall, 1874. The street is cobbled and pointing down it, from between the imposing double-flight of steps to the 1761-built Guildhall, is a Crimean War cannon, brought home from the siege of Sebastopol, 1854-55.

Holes Bay and Poole Old Town, from the air, about 1930. Seen from Hamworthy, with pottery kilns on the site of what is now the power station (near right), looking across the Back Water Channel of Holes Bay to West Quay. Midway along there is a ship of some size, about 150 feet length, berthed beside the boatyard.

OPPOSITE
Poole Old Town, about 1915. Pedlar in St Aubyn's Court, one of the narrow streets in the shadow of St James's church.

Thames Alley, 1969. Georgian walls and roofs, with cobbles, plus an early twentieth century gas-lamp cast with the town's dolphin emblem. This was the heart of the Old Town.

Church Street, 1969. Demolitions had gone too far in the 1960s, leading to the ultimate irony of mock-Georgian rebuilding that attempted to match what had stood there before.

Poole Park

Poole Park, 1890s. Older oaks amongst the saplings and new paths of the forty acres of pleasure grounds that were laid out in 1885-89.

495. POOLE PARK

Poole Park, 1920s. All was now quiet on the Western Front and in Dorset one of its field guns was a curiosity for the new generation.

Poole Park, 1920s. The tennis courts, with two of the younger spectators finding the cameraman a source of greater interest.

Tennis in Poole Park. P9.

Longfleet

Longfleet, 1969. The new Poole General Hospital, opened by Her Majesty Queen Elizabeth II and the Duke of Edinburgh on 11 July that year. Behind it is the tower of St Mary's church, rebuilt in 1914-15.

OPPOSITE, top
Bournemouth Road, Parkstone, about 1910. Tramcar No.30, from the Square at Bournemouth, en route to Poole Park.

OPPOSITE
Constitution Hill, about 1910. The view down North Road, with the tram, and across what was then the village of Parkstone, to Poole Harbour and the Purbeck Hills.

Parkstone

POOLE AND HARBOUR FROM CONSTITUTION HILL

Parkstone Golf Links, about 1915. The view up Luscombe Valley, from The Bluff, with Lilliput Road crossing the picture in the middle distance.

Parkstone Park, 1890s. Though only three acres, it gave a green focal point to the new suburb. The centre path ringed a terracotta fountain and the lawns were well endowed with trees.

South Western Pottery, Parkstone, 1962. Half a mile south of Parkstone Station, South Western Pottery had its own standard gauge tramway which came off a siding immediately west of the station. Its engine, the saddle tank 'George Jennings', was bought in 1902 and scrapped in 1964. In the early twentieth century this mineral line extended a mile further south, to Salterns Pier on the Main Channel of Poole Harbour at Lilliput.

Branksome Heath School, Livingstone Road, Parkstone, 1921. Classes I and II.

Branksome Park

Branksome Dene Chine, Bournemouth.

Branksome Dene Chine, 1920s. The eastern extremity of Poole's seaboard, with the last bit of sand before it could be officially claimed by Bournemouth. Despite the new café and the beach-huts this was still a wild place, replete with legends of smuggling days.

OPPOSITE
Branksome Park, about 1910. 'The hills at Parkstone are clothed with trees of the fir tribe, which afford shelter from the wind and secure an equable climate, and here a number of good resi-dences have been erected,' to quote Kelly's Directory of Dorsetshire.

Branksome Chine

SNOW SCENE, BRANKSOME LAKES, BOURNE

Branksome Chine, about 1910. Summer and winter views of the lakes, in the forty acres of gardens between Western Road and Lakeside Road that were given to Poole Corporation by the Bury Estate trustees in 1895.

Branksome Towers, 1970s. View seawards from one of Britain's more desirable tower-blocks, redeveloped by Elliott Property.

OPPOSITE, top
Branksome Chine, 1927. Tacky collection of huts and cars, two of whose drivers have ignored the instruction to 'Please Park Cars This Side of Board'. Behind it (centre left) stands a rustic thatched cabin – the café.

OPPOSITE
Branksome Chine, 1977. Car park, Solarium, a few remaining beach-huts, and the sand now disciplined with a promenade and a series of groynes, stretching eastwards to Bournemouth.

Canford Cliffs

SIMPSON's FOLLY. 1881

Simpson's Folly, Canford Cliffs, 1881. Built by an old sea captain, in 1878, the house upon the sand had already been undermined by the sea. Visitors covered the walls with texts and proverbs.

Simpson's Folly, Canford Cliffs, 1892. The Biblical warning about building upon sand had come to pass, with the aid of explosives after it had become unsafe.

Simpson's Folly, Canford Cliffs, about 1910. Blown up by gunpowder, around 1890, its heap of eroding concrete remained visible at the water's edge until 1946. The promenade was extended across its site in 1961.

Canford Cliffs, about 1910. Edwardian villas line the sea front at Cliff Drive.

Canford Cliffs, 1960s. The view south, against the light and across what has since proved to be an oil-rich Poole Bay, to the chalk stacks at Old Harry Rocks and the line of Ballard Down in the Purbeck Hills.

OPPOSITE
Invasion 1940. Southern Command had its Camouflage School at Poole, and prepared Canford Cliffs for the arrival of Hitler's Operation Sealion.

Compton Acres, Canford Cliffs, 1980s. Several private gardens on the west side of Canford Cliffs Road have been linked to provide a remarkable mixture of classical and oriental taste, plus some exotic species.

OPPOSITE, top

Sandbanks, about 1915. 'Life at The Sandbanks' this postcard was captioned. 'The Sandbanks' was how the peninsula of sand dunes was known in its pioneer days.

OPPOSITE

Sandbanks, about 1930. Looking north along Banks Road and across North Haven Lake to Lilliput. Banks Road was metalled in 1924-26 in a scheme to alleviate unemployment.

Sandbanks

LIFE AT THE SANDBANKS.

Sand Banks. Poole. P4

The Sandbanks Hotel, 1940. Requisitioned by the army, and with the name over its gate removed in accordance with Defence Regulations, this was the School for Junior Leaders. They are seen exercising in the tennis court, removing the half-track from a Bren-gun carrier, and leaping into the sand dunes to stuff bayonets into dummy Germans.

Sandbanks, about 1930. The view north-east from Salter Road, showing the isthmus, with Poole Harbour to the left and Poole Bay to the right.

Sandbanks Ferry, 1930s. Approach of the 'Floating Bridge', a vehicular chain-ferry, from the Isle of Purbeck, and an open passenger boat preparing to leave for Shell Bay, on the other side of the harbour mouth. The chain-ferry started running in 1926.

Sandbanks, 1980s. Seen from above Brownsea Island, and its castle, in a view across the Main Channel of Poole Harbour. The tapering isthmus (top left) connects the Sandbanks with the mainland at Lilliput. At the opposite end of the peninsula is the mouth of the harbour. The rounded shoreline facing Brownsea is North Haven Point.

Creekmoor, about 1955. 'Fojo' working the Creekmoor Light Railway. The major complex of industrial buildings beside Soper's Lane had been a wartime munitions plant, producing Oerlikon machine guns.

OPPOSITE
Holes Bay, 1970s. The railway across this northern arm of Poole Harbour was constructed in 1893 and became the mainline from Weymouth to Poole and Bournemouth. The train carries the route number 91.

Broadstone

Broadstone, about 1935. Looking north from the Roman Road at the expanding district that had sprung up where the road from Poole to Blandford bridged the railway junction, which from 1845 to 1893 was the area's closest connection for London.

Broadstone Station, 1972. This right-hand set of track, looking south towards Upton and Hamworthy, was built from Wimborne in 1845. It provided Poole's first trains, in a circuitous service that was dubbed Castleman's Corkscrew. The track between the other two platforms headed for Creekmoor and Poole's present railway station. This was added with the building of the Poole Junction Railway in 1872-74. Dereliction came with Dr Richard Beeching's cuts.

OPPOSITE   Broadstone Junction, 7 August 1954. Somerset and Dorset 7F engine, 2-8-0 number 53808, with the 7.43 am Saturday service from Birmingham New Street, nearing the end of its journey to Bournemouth West. Looking north, with the train crossing the points from the Western Loop, constructed in 1885 to by-pass Wimborne. The carriages are seen coming off this line, which forked off the original Somerset and Dorset track at Corfe Mullen. Behind the third carriage, and on to which the engine has just crossed, is the 1845-built line of Castleman's Corkscrew. It came from Wimborne via Oakley and Merley. As for the engine, this large-boilered locomotive was built in 1925 and originally carried Somerset and Dorset number 89. She was withdrawn in the mid-1960s and delivered to Barry scrapyard, South Wales, for breaking up. There the story might have ended, but 53808 was bought in 1970 by the Somerset and Dorset Railway Museum Trust, and returned to Somerset for restoration.

Broadstone, 1970s. Now a suburb of Poole, its housing estates continue to spread across former gravel pits and into the remnants of heathland.